Deliver Outstanding Customer Service

Gain and retain customers and stay
ahead of the competition

SUSAN NASH and DEREK NASH

2nd edition

Originally published in 2000 as
Exceeding Customer Expectations

Published in 2002 by
How To Books Ltd, 3 Newtec Place,
Magdalen Road, Oxford OX4 1RE, United Kingdom
Tel: (01865) 793806   Fax: (01865) 248780

British Library Cataloguing in Publication Data
A catalogue record for this book is available from
the British Library

Edited by Diana Brueton
Cover design by Baseline Arts Ltd., Oxford

Produced for How To Books by Deer Park Productions
Typeset by Anneset, Weston-super-Mare, Somerset
Printed and bound in Great Britain

NOTE: The material contained in this book is set out in good
faith for general guidance and no liability can be accepted
for loss or expense incurred as a result of relying in particular
circumstances on statements made in the book. The laws and
regulations are complex and liable to change, and readers should
check the current position with the relevant authorities before
making personal arrangements.

Contents

List of illustrations

Preface

You have the best-quality, feature-rich product on the market, you have hired top talent from across the industry, and yet your company is not performing as it should. Why?

Maybe customer needs are not being met, or the customer does not feel valued. You may have forgotten that often the critical competitive edge in becoming a market leader is reached by exceeding customers' expectations. As business enters the 21st century, customer service remains a fundamental factor for business success and profitability.

The reasons for this are many, but we will focus on two. First, customers' expectations have risen: 'mass class' prevails where more goods and services are available, to more people, for less cost than ever before. Second, customers have fewer opportunities to receive personal service than even ten years ago: witness the automated tellers, the decline of home delivery, the growth of internet malls, etc. So when the customer has an opportunity to receive service from an organisation, they often have a pent-up need for human interaction.

The combination of these two factors makes delivering exceptional service as important today as ever before. As a result, some organisations leap on the customer service bandwagon. They produce fancy slogans, offer incentives and train their people, often to no avail. Why? Because exceeding customers' expectations involves company-wide change that needs constant reinforcement and effort. It requires a consistent process of efforts – it is not an event.

Who should read this book?

This book is designed for anyone who is working within an organisation, whether small or large, who wants to improve standards of service to the customer. Whether you are a business owner, manager, service provider or executive, this book will provide useful tools and techniques to improve service at all levels in your organisation.

What is the purpose of this book?

The purpose of this book is to provide a methodology to systematically improve the service provided to customers so that customer expectations can be exceeded and your business can remain viable.

Using this book

In this book we introduce a service management model with specific tools and techniques within each section:

In Chapters 1 and 2 we define customer service in some depth, and describe a comprehensive approach to improving it. Based on your own assessment of your needs, you then choose which chapters to tackle next.

In Chapters 3 to 10 you will be given information, skills and techniques to raise your competency in specific areas where you may need help. Each chapter includes examples, exercises, case studies and discussion points to enable you to directly apply the principles introduced to help improve service to your customers. Embedded in each chapter are ideas for 'keeping the fires alive': many organisations make a great start, only to lose momentum and focus, resulting in service deteriorating, employees becoming disillusioned (more 'smile' training) and customers becoming dissatisfied.

The outcome of implementing these ideas can be creating situations where you are able to delight the customer: to provide a service that far exceeds the customers' expectations. These situations become the stories that act as free PR and build a company's reputation. We will close the book by sharing a few of these stories, to highlight what you can expect to see when the entire customer service strategy comes to fruition.

The contents of this book were developed after many years of working with a broad range of organisations as they struggled to make delivering outstanding customer service a fact and not a fantasy. Good luck in this journey!

CHAPTER 1

Understanding Customer Service

W hile most of us deal with customer service every day, either as a customer or as a service provider, many of us do not necessarily understand what constitutes good customer service. To a certain extent we are not aware of the factors that make us satisfied or dissatisfied. In this chapter we will lay the groundwork for the rest of the book by identifying some misconceptions about the critical components of a positive service interaction, and then by thoroughly defining customer service.

Customer service quiz

To raise awareness and to set the scene for the rest of this chapter, take a moment and answer the following questions. For each question, circle the answer you think is correct. Circle only one answer for each question. Think about customer service in general, for instance in banks, restaurants, retail stores, etc, not necessarily the context in which you provide customer service.

1. What is the biggest single reason why businesses lose customers?
    a   new competition
    b   indifference of one employee
    c   word of mouth
    d   dissatisfaction with the product.

2. What percent of dissatisfied customers *do not* complain to you about discourteous or indifferent customer service?
    a   48%
    b   65%
    c   78%
    d   96%.

3. Of those customers who do complain, what percent is likely to return to that business again?
    a   50%
    b   70%
    c   80%
    d   90%.

4. For the average business, what percent of annual sales comes from existing satisfied customers?
    a   30%
    b   10%
    c   65%
    d   50%.

5. How much more money does it take to find a new customer instead of getting more business from an existing one?
    a   twice as much
    b   three times as much
    c   four times as much
    d   over five times as much.

6. A dissatisfied customer will tell how many people, outside of the company, about poor service received?
    a   two or three people
    b   four to six people
    c   seven to eight people
    d   over nine people, but as many as 20.

Customer service quiz answers

1. b
2. d
3. d
4. c
5. d
6. d

(Gathered from TARP research conducted by the White House Office of Consumer Affairs and quoted in *How to Win Customers and Keep Them for Life* by Michael Le Boeuf.)

Why customers leave (question 1)

The biggest single reason why businesses lose customers is:
- Indifference of one employee – 68 per cent.

Other reasons customers choose to take their business elsewhere are:
- Dissatisfaction with the product – 14 per cent.
- New competition – 9 per cent.
- Word of mouth – 5 per cent.

This research was based on answers from customers who were asked: 'What was the factor that influenced your decision not to use this product or service again?' At the point of interaction between the customer and the service provider, the indifference of one employee was cited as the major reason customers chose to take their business elsewhere.

> Every individual within a company can make a significant impact, not only on the customer experience, but also on the company's service reputation in the marketplace.

Obviously, businesses have to offer a comparable, competitive product that is technically adequate in order to ensure the long-term viability of the organisation. Amdahl was renowned for providing exceptional customer service, but was unable to change its approach from being a mainframe supplier to supplying a product geared towards the distributed environment. Many responsible for providing customer service question this data, as they believe product quality is the deciding influence. Later in this chapter, that is one myth we will dispel.

Who complains (question 2)?

Ninety-six per cent of dissatisfied customers *do not* complain to you about discourteous or indifferent customer service: we only hear from 4 per cent of our dissatisfied customers. This means that for every complaint received, there are in fact 26 other customers with problems, six of which are serious issues.

The rest either vote with their feet, and do not return, or complain to anyone else *outside* the company who will listen.

> In order to deliver exceptional service, we have to create the means for customers to complain to us.

Only when we know about the problems will we be able to resolve them. The concept of providing our customers with the tools they can use to complain, and recovering from the complaint, is covered in later chapters.

After complaining, who returns (question 3)?

Of those customers who do complain, what percent is likely to return to that business again? Interestingly enough complainers are more likely than non-complainers to do business with the company that upset them, even if the problem is not satisfactorily resolved. However, this question has two correct answers. If the complaint is not handled effectively, only 50 per cent of customers will do business with that organisation again. When British Airways conducted their initial market research into customer perceptions, it showed that when the service delivery was acceptable, the customers were satisfied. However, when a problem occurred only 50 per cent of the customers would return to the airline, based on the fact that their complaint was not resolved to their satisfaction. They termed this process of successfully resolving customer complaints as 'recovery'. If the complaint was resolved quickly and successfully, over 95 per cent of customers would return. Effective recovery is an incredibly important service management tool.

> When customers complain, they are doing so because they care and want to continue to do business with the organisation.

The successful resolution of complaints is such a novel experience, that achieving results in this area can drastically impact customer loyalty. Chapter 7 will discuss strategies for recovery in more detail.

Service and sales (question 4)

The most conservative data infers that over 65 per cent of annual sales comes from existing satisfied customers. The figures are even higher in some service businesses and when adding the factor of referrals.

> Some businesses receive almost 100 per cent of their new business from existing satisfied customers and the referrals they make to others.

Consulting firms often get most of their business this way.

Cost of generating new business (question 5)

Research in this area has produced different results.

> Estimates show that it costs five to ten times as much to generate business from new customers as it does to get more business from existing customers.

Despite this data, companies continue to invest large amounts of promotional money to encourage new customers to try their service or product, and then ruin the experience at the service delivery point! If a problem arises, customers are often turned over to a 'customer service department' that does not have the authority to correct the problem. An alternative strategy would be to invest the money used for promotion to improve the overall service delivery process – a more economical and long-term option.

Spreading the word (question 6)

The 'average' customer who has a problem tells nine to ten people about it. Approximately 13 per cent of unsatisfied customers will tell more than 20 people, personally, about the problem. Of the people they tell, each one will on average tell two to three more people. This means that usually 200–300 people personally hear about every negative service experience. A scary thought, particularly when you combine the effect of the Internet where potentially 100 million people could read about the same customer service horror story!

Conversely good news does not travel as fast as bad news. On average, a satisfied customer will only tell three to five people about the experience.

> You have to deliver much more good service to outweigh the possible negative consequences of bad service.

Conclusions

Of the six questions, how many did you answer correctly? In our research we have found that, on average, most people answer between three and four questions accurately.

From this you can see that most of us need to broaden our understanding of customer service. Let's begin to define customer service in more detail.

Factors that make us satisfied or dissatisfied

What constitutes positive or negative customer service?

Hotels are renowned for confusing bookings. When travelling recently, the room key I was given wouldn't work because someone else was already in the room. When I went back to reception the response I was given was 'the system made a mistake!' The factors that made me dissatisfied with that experience were:

- ◆ no ownership of the problem
- ◆ no apology
- ◆ blaming of the mistake onto someone/thing else
- ◆ no resolution of the problem
- ◆ couldn't-care-less attitude.

Exercise   Think of your own experiences as a customer, in retail, restaurants, hotels, travel, etc. Think of a specific time when you were dissatisfied with the service you received. How did you feel? What factors contributed to your dissatisfaction? Try to separate the experience itself from the factors that caused you to feel the service did not meet your expectations. List the factors associated with your negative experience.

On another visit to a hotel in Denver, my room reservation was once again confused, but with a twist. This time, someone else was given a key to the room I was in! A poor, tired business executive walked into the room and found an undressed woman cleaning her teeth. He exited the room much quicker than he entered! Thirty seconds later there was another knock at the door. The front desk manager had come up to personally apologise for the mistake and to reassure me that it would not happen again. In addition, the following evening there was a personal note from the front desk manager apologising for the disturbance accompanied by a bottle of wine and a basket of cheese and crackers.

The factors that made this a satisfactory experience were:

- ownership of the problem
- apology
- exceeding expectations – free wine!
- personalised service
- speed of response
- positive attitude
- no blaming of systems.

Now think of a specific time when you were satisfied with the service you received. The experience could be in retail, restaurants, hotels, travel, etc. How did you feel? What factors contributed to your satisfaction? Try to separate the experience itself from the factors that caused you to feel the service exceeded your expectations. List the factors that contributed to your satisfaction.

We will return to these ideas when we have described in more detail the two types of service.

Material and personal service

There are two types of service: *material and personal.*
Material service, or the content part of service, consists of price, timing, quality and quantity of:

- equipment
- products
- physical comfort
- delivery
- procedures
- routines
- staffing
- information
- definition of roles and responsibilities.

Material service relates to the tangible parts of the service delivery process. For airlines it comprises the size and age of planes, food, baggage handling, booking systems, etc. For retail organisations the material service comprises the storefront, display cases, inventory, cash registers, product information, etc. For hotels, the material service comprises the bedrooms, the bathroom facilities, the storage space, the equipment provided, the telephone service, etc.

Exercise | If you are in the service delivery business, what are the material service aspects of your product?

Personal service consists of the interpersonal aspects in providing service, which include:

- body language
- verbal communication
- using the customer's name
- giving your undivided attention
- showing respect for the individual
- being calm and confident.

Personal service relates to the intangible aspects of providing your product or service. These are harder to measure, control and manage because they take place at the moment of the interaction, cannot be standardised and vary from one moment to another – personal service is *situational*. What is acceptable to one customer one day may be unacceptable to the same customer on another day, because of differing circumstances.

For airlines the personal service comprises the greeting, the way the check-in staff interact with the customer, the amount of eye contact, etc. For retail organisations the personal service comprises the effectiveness of the sales person in establishing rapport, identifying customer needs, suggesting appropriate products and describing them in customer-friendly terms, etc. For hotels, the personal service comprises such things as the friendliness of the check-in, the ability of the staff to answer questions about the hotel and its facilities, the ability to respond to non-standard questions, etc.

Exercise	If you are in the service delivery business, what are the personal service aspects of your product?

Research on material and personal service

Material service is the easiest to define, measure and compare. When complaints are received or market research conducted, it is more likely that the easily defined points of material service will be commented on. When Jan Carlzon, the Chief Executive Officer of Scandinavian Airlines (SAS) took over SAS in 1981, the airline was not popular with airline travellers. He conducted market research and found that customers said they wanted the material service of the airline to be improved – bigger planes, more legroom, quicker baggage handling and better food. At the same time he came across in a library, research conducted in the US.

The library example: first group

To conduct research two groups were used. For the first group the librarian was told that she was in the book-stamping business, not to be rude but to move the customers through the check-out quickly and efficiently. These customers were interviewed when they left the library. Initially somewhat reluctant to be interviewed, their comments on the service they had received included:

- The library was dark.
- It was hard to find the books.
- The library was unwelcoming.
- Overall they were dissatisfied with the service experience.
- No one mentioned the librarian.

The library example: second group

For the second group, the librarian was told to do three things:

1 Use the customer's name (it was on the card, so not a complicated request).
2 Smile (they were told to not be effusive but since it uses more muscles than a frown it's good exercise).
3 Touch the customer's hand as he/she passed the book back

(due to increased sensitivity to sexual harassment, we only recommend using the first two).

These customers were also interviewed as they left the library. This group seemed more willing to be interviewed and made the following comments on the service they had received:

- The library was warm.
- The filing system was easy to understand.
- The lighting and ventilation was good.
- Overall they were satisfied with the service experience.
- No one mentioned the librarian.

The library example: conclusions

Although the customers commented on the *material* aspects of the service, the differentiating factor, and the only thing that had changed, was the *personal* service the customers had received.

When Jan Carlzon heard about this research, he decided instead of initially investing in new aeroplanes, better food, etc (the material aspects), to invest in training the people in the airline on how to provide personalised service to each customer. He invested in a two-day programme called Personal Service through Personal Development that was offered to all his 12,000 employees. The results, as they say, are history. Passengers started to comment on the improvement in flying SAS, and the consequent increase in credibility and passenger flow enabled Jan Carlzon to invest in some of the more important material aspects of service. This approach was then adopted by British Airways, who also implemented this 'wall-to-wall' training that we will discuss in a later chapter.

Exercise   Revisit the factors that made you satisfied and dissatisfied. Go back to the lists of factors that made you satisfied and those that made you dissatisfied. Mark the factors that represent personal service with a P and material service with an M. Some factors, such as lack of product information, could be a combination of both personal and material factors. Review the list and identify which factors appear most often – personal or material. Most lists have more personal than material service factors.

Material and personal service

To summarise, if material service is up to standard it has, at best, a neutral effect on the customer. In planning their service policies, most companies focus on the material aspect. In the training of personnel it is frequently the working method, technical competence and routine that are accentuated. The personal aspect is often overlooked.

> Personal service is a key element that contributes to customer satisfaction and long-term customer loyalty.

When you think of restaurants where you like to eat or hotels where you like to stay it's often the personal service that provides the greater reason for you to return.

If a customer receives satisfactory material service, but poor personal service, the service is often described as bad or unsatisfactory. If a customer receives poor material service, but excellent personal service the service is often perceived as good or satisfactory.

As we move on to deciding how to deliver oustanding customer sevice, it is important to ensure that material service processes and procedures are adequate and not preventing service providers from meeting customer needs. However, a greater emphasis will be placed on how to establish and ensure consistent personal service – the factor that makes or breaks the customer's perception of the service delivered.

Internal and external service

Too frequently we think of customer service as an *external* activity: something that occurs outside the organisation to keep paying customers happy. But *internal customer service* is equally important. Serving the people we work with, and doing everything we can to help them do their job well, is critical to the organisation's success.

Internal customer service

Internal customer service means treating your colleagues as if they were your paying customers. It means delivering competent, quality work in a courteous and helpful manner. It's doing something extra for your colleagues: taking that extra time or expending that extra energy.

We're all internal customers. We depend on each other for ideas, services and materials. We all have customers and we are all customers. Internal customer service is the same as external customer service; it just applies to the people within the company rather than outside it.

Good internal service is important because:

◆ Internal customer service instils a spirit of cooperation and teamwork in your organisation. Everyone feels this is a great place to work.

◆ Internal customer service helps everyone produce top-quality work . . . on time and within budget.

◆ Internal customer service will help your company, and you, to grow.

◆ Internal customer service helps you feel better about your job. You'll enjoy what you do even more.

The relationship between good internal and external customer service

Working together, people and departments, is what good internal customer service is about. And when you treat your colleagues as you would like to be treated, and they do the same in return, you reach your full potential and so does the organisation.

Your external customers are only satisfied with the best service and/or product. It's only by working together internally that the best can be achieved. External customer service often mirrors internal customer service.

Service pyramid

Service delivery requires an alternative organisational structure based on an inverted pyramid, with three levels: *service providers*, *service support* and *management*.

– Service providers who have direct interaction with the customer.

– Service support personnel who provide important internal services so that service providers can meet customer needs.

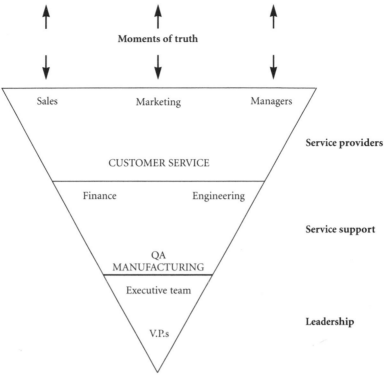

Fig. 1.   The service pyramid.

  – Management/leaders who are there to provide vital support for the service initiative.

Let's look at a situation in technical support, where the customer wants their product/application repaired.

Service providers

There are several departments that have direct interaction with the customer. The employees who work in these departments are called service providers and include:

- Those who answer the phone – first-level support.
- Those who initially try to fix the problem – second-level support.
- Those to whom the problem is sent if it can't be fixed – third-level support.
- Managers who may get involved when a customer is irate.
- Sales personnel who told the customer that the product would meet their needs.

Service support

There are many departments within organisations that service providers depend on to meet customer needs. These functional areas are called service support. Some are obvious, and some are more subtle in their contribution to customer satisfaction. The less obvious ones include:

◆ Engineers dedicated to providing more advanced support to customers and software code fixes.

◆ Engineers in development.

◆ Quality assurance to ensure products don't have bugs in the first place.

◆ Purchasing to ensure there are materials to construct the product.

◆ Finance to ensure there is adequate cash flow.

◆ Human resources to ensure people are hired who can design the product.

◆ Shipping to ensure the product reaches the customer.

The list goes on and on and any of these departments can negatively influence customer service. Yet often these groups do not perceive themselves to be in the role of service provider, or may be on the receiving end of conflicting priorities (your job is to get out new products, not just fix existing products). To consistently deliver outstanding customer service everyone in the organisation needs to be focused on the customer. Chapter 7 will describe how service level agreements are a tool to ensure internal customers are committed to meeting external customer needs.

Managers/leaders

The final component of delivering exceptional service is provided by support from senior management. Contrary to traditional organisation charts, managers, directors, vice presidents and presidents are there to support the service delivery process. If they don't 'walk the walk', customer service can't be anything other than a buzzword. Often after managers review the service delivery methodology presented in Chapter 2 they realise that it is a difficult process and don't want to make the commitment required to institute a customer service culture. As a result customer service becomes a platitude, not a strategy, and therefore will not succeed.

Exercise	Who is responsible for helping the customer? Select a specific customer service transaction that has taken place with your company. Begin with the outcome and then trace the transaction back through the company to identify which are service providers, which are required to support the service and the role of managers in interactions with the customers, using the following categories:

♦ brief description of the situation
♦ service providers
♦ service support
♦ managers.

Think about the extent to which each department is focused on meeting customer needs. What internal barriers exist that might prevent service providers from delivering oustanding customer service?

Moments of truth

The phrase *moments of truth* represents a powerful idea for helping people in service businesses shift their point of view and think about the customer's experience. A moment of truth represents the critical interaction a customer has with an organisation. Jan Carlzon used the phrase to great effect when he described the airline as having 50,000 moments of truth every day. Managing service means managing the moments of truth, so as many as possible turn out positively.

> A moment of truth is any point in the interaction during which the customer has an opportunity to gain an impression of the service provided by the company.

Some moments of truth are created by systems – no map given of a hotel layout at check in. Some moments of truth are created by interaction with personnel from the company: asking a question and receiving a complete and thorough answer.

Every moment of truth is not created equal; some have a stronger ability to influence the customer's perception of the service. For instance, if the customer is irate and the problem is resolved to their satisfaction, this moment of truth will be given greater weight by the customer in describing the service experience. Unexpected positive moments of truth will also influence the customer's perception of the service – being greeted with a smile walking through hotel corridors by a hotel employee, the use of their name when leaving a restaurant.

The examples of poor customer service you listed in the exercise earlier in this chapter represent *dull moments of truth*. These are those critical interactions that leave the customer feeling negative, disappointed, unpleasantly surprised and therefore dissatisfied with the customer service.

The examples of good customer service represent *shining moments of truth*. These are those critical interactions that leave the customer feeling positive, enthusiastic, pleasantly surprised and therefore satisfied with the customer service.

> Research has shown that it takes, on average, 12 *shining moments of truth* to compensate for one *dull moment of truth*.

Service summarised

As we have seen, service is more complex than simply being a task completed by a customer service department. Service is:

- ◆ To a large extent, intangible: it cannot be reproduced as a concrete object and it can vary from one moment to the next.
- ◆ Situational: what is positive for one customer one day, and meets their expectations, may be perceived differently by the same customer on another day and fail to meet expectations.
- ◆ Difficult to measure: one of the ironies of customer service is that the higher you set expectation by delivering exceptional service, the more the customers expect the next time they deal with you. So you may provide better service than a competitor, but because of differing expectations the customer may be satisfied with the competitor's service but not with yours. (Compare your expectations of a meal in a fast food restaurant

to one in a high class hotel. A smile would be a great service from the fast food restaurant, but you would expect considerably more from the hotel.)

◆ Subjective: what is acceptable for one customer may be totally unacceptable to another. Depending on people's awareness of service, standards will vary from one individual to another.

◆ Influenced by the service provider: if the service provider sets expectations effectively, the customer will probably be satisfied. If the service provider sets expectations ineffectively and fails to meet them, the customer will probably not be satisfied. For instance, if you tell the customer you will call at 3 pm and you call at 5 pm, you have not met customer expectations. If you tell the customer you will call the next day, and you call at 5 pm the same day, you have just exceeded the expectations. The same action, but with a differing set of expectations, produces a different level of customer satisfaction.

> Don't over-promise and under-deliver. Make sure you under-promise and over-deliver.

◆ A component in every product a company makes and distributes: there are no companies that just produce products. Even an organisation such as Amazon.com that sells books over the Internet has service components: a 'thank you' e-mail after an order is placed, a reminder about new releases proactively sent, etc.

◆ Not just in industries categorised within certain SEC codes: there is a service component in every customer offering, it just depends what percentage is tangible product and what percentage is service.

◆ Not provided by a customer service department alone. In the next chapter we will introduce a model, based on this definition of service, for improving service delivery. First, however, let's meet the three companies we will be studying as they implement a customer service improvement strategy in order to try to consistently exceed customer expectations.

Case Studies: Who is Cleanworks?

Cleanworks is not even a real company yet – it is a concept that comes to fruition and becomes an organisation by the end of the book.

The concept of Cleanworks arose from market research undertaken by a major soap manufacturer and distributor. With a stable market and shrinking margins, the company wished to diversify from its core business into new, possibly more lucrative service opportunities. It created a department whose charter was to identify potential new openings that would capitalise on the organisation's strengths, yet would provide greater growth and long-term profit potential.

Research focused on the company's core market and spread into the laundry and dry cleaning market. This market was not only highly diversified, with no major national or international organisations, but also filled with dissatisfied customers and poor service levels. Combined with this, research indicated that people were struggling with too much to do in too little time, and were therefore gravitating even more towards service businesses to create more leisure time. The advent of 'mass class' was indicated by the growth of such companies as Starbucks, John Lewis Partnership, Home Depot, Pottery Barn, etc. Mass class is the making available of better quality products to a wider audience through standard delivery channels. Cleanworks was identified as a possible laundry and dry cleaning business that would undertake home delivery, thereby providing people with more time. They would also provide exemplary service, and capitalise on economies of scale to standardise this highly diverse market. The company decided initially that it would build a plant and the business from scratch, rather than trying to change the culture of an acquired company.

Case Study: Who is Kitchen Barn?

Kitchen Barn is a division of a large, national speciality retailer who currently uses two distribution channels: mail order and retail stores. Kitchen Barn has been one of four divisions of its parent company ever since it was purchased in 1988. In the past year there has been a push to reposition Kitchen Barn in a different market niche, as a more up-scale retailer, with larger stores and higher-priced merchandise, including furniture. The parent organisation has always had a reputation for providing good customer service, but the new direction and increased competition in the marketplace have combined to raise awareness to focus on delivering outstanding customer service. We will follow this organisation as it 'restarts' its customer focus campaign.

Case Study: Who is Internet Express?

Internet Express is a software company providing services on the web. The company was created by the merger of two larger organisations two years ago, and since then has grown to its current size by acquiring five more companies. As a result there was not one unifying culture, but a combination of several different ones. Network Logic had a slower-paced, customer-focused approach, but this had resulted in a long product development cycle and a loss of market status. MacDonald software had a more 'get out and make it happen' culture, with shorter product development cycles and less focus on customer loyalty. Neither culture respected or valued what the other brought to the table. The combination of these two diverse cultures, with the often-hostile cultures of the companies that were taken over, resulted in a somewhat unproductive work environment, and as a result spotty customer service. In this case study we will follow the Vice President of Technical Support as he integrates several different technical support structures and tries to raise overall service levels to the customer._____

Discussion points

1. Based on the factors that made you satisfied or dissatisfied as a customer, what influence did material and personal service have on you? Are you more product-focused or relationship-focused?

2. To what extent have you defined the material and personal service you provide to your external customers? What are the most important facets of your material service? How well do you provide exceptional personal service?

3. How positive are the interactions between the differing departments in your company? What internal barriers exist that might affect customer service levels? Which departments appear customer-focused and which appear product-focused?

4. To what extent is the customer focus reflected throughout your company? How traditional is your organisation structure? To what extent do those in the service support functions view customer service as part of their responsibility?

5. What do you think are the most important moments of truth that your team, group, company faces every day?

6. What percentage of your business is concrete, tangible, product-based, and what percentage is service-based?

Summary

In this chapter you have been given a comprehensive definition of customer service that will act as a building block for the rest of the book. You learned the following about customer service:

- From completing the customer service quiz, you probably realised you don't know as much about customer service as you might have thought.
- There are two types of service:
  - Material, relating to the content part of the service delivery process.
  - Personal, relating to the interpersonal aspects of serving the customer.
- The way the employees treat each other internally (internal customer service) is important for providing exceptional service to external customers. The inverted service delivery pyramid provides a model for how this approach can be implemented and understood within organisations.
- To deliver outstanding customer service you need to optimise as many 'moments of truth' as possible with customers. Moments of truth represent the critical point where the organisation and its people interact with the customer; the moments can be small (how the customer is greeted) or large (completing a major project).
- In addition we realised that customer service is intangible, subjective, situational, and can be influenced by the service provider and every organisation provides some elements of service in its product mix.
- In short, consistently delivering outstanding customer service relies upon a complex company-wide approach, rather than trying to establish or improve a customer service department.

CHAPTER 2

Delivering Outstanding Customer Service

A s we saw in the previous chapter, many of us have an unclear understanding of what customer service really is. It's not surprising, therefore, that when organisations try to raise customer service levels many of their efforts appear unsuccessful. In this chapter we will provide a *service management model* to show what is required to consistently deliver outstanding customer service. We will also take some time to show *how to evaluate current customer service levels*. It's hard to improve if you don't know from whence you started! Finally we will revisit our case studies to show how each company established its service management approach and prioritised its plan of attack.

Service management model

In order to effectively manage moments of truth, applying a service management model is essential. Based on the model originally developed for British Airways and incorporating a continuous improvement philosophy, the process defines critical activities necessary to ensure consistent excellent service delivery in five specific areas:

1. Establishing a clear customer service strategy.
2. Ensuring the correct people are in place, with the correct skills to deliver outstanding personal service.
3. Establishing clear material service delivery processes.
4. Improving continuously in terms of process improvement, quality monitoring and recovery.
5. Management playing a key daily part in acting as role models for the delivery of these principles.

By implementing certain important milestones in all five categories it is possible to optimise the critical moments of truth for both personal and material service in the entire service delivery process (see Figure 2).

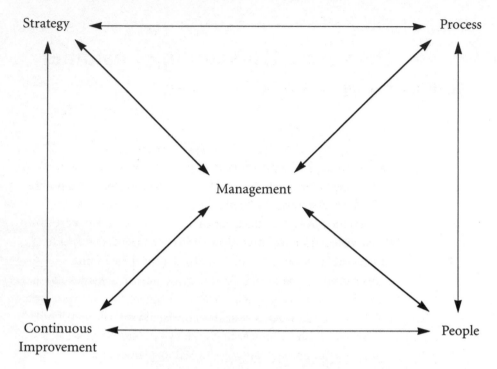

Fig. 2.   The service management model.

Establishing a customer service strategy

To establish a clear customer service strategy certain key actions are required:

◆ understanding the overall organisational vision and mission
◆ defining the organisation's customer service direction
◆ creating the organisation's customer service slogan
◆ establishing the organisation's customer service values
◆ ensuring customer service is defined as a key responsibility for the business/department
◆ communicating the customer service standards and vision.

An outcome of this process is often a communications programme for all staff, including but not limited to:

◆ publishing the customer service visions/standards in posters, newsletters, badges, etc
◆ communicating the customer service vision through small group meetings
◆ establishing an event for the entire group/company to launch

and clarify the customer service philosophy (see psychology of service in Chapter 5).

Hiring, training and keeping the right people

Ensuring the right people are in place, with the correct skills to deliver outstanding personal service, requires:

- Hiring the right people. This is achieved by:
  - defining job requirements
  - using behavioural interviewing skills to evaluate against the defined job requirements
  - conducting assessment centres.
- Providing training in key areas required to deliver exceptional personal service.
- Providing ongoing coaching and feedback on personal service skills.
- Motivating employees to produce outstanding results.

Managing the material service delivery processes

This critical step involves defining, reviewing and improving service delivery processes and procedures. This requires:

- Mapping the service delivery processes.
- Evaluating critical success points in the process.
- Establishing service delivery procedures to optimise material service.
- Creating service level agreements.

Instituting continuous improvement processes

- Continuous improvement involves reinforcing and adapting both personal and material service delivery processes on an ongoing basis.
- Actions used to reinforce personal service standards are the designing and building of follow-up tools and activities to aid retention.

Sample approaches include:

- establishing customer focus teams
- ongoing reinforcement activities such as meetings, newsletters, etc

  - creating reward systems
  - further training.
- ◆ Actions used to reinforce material service standards are:
  - applying problem-solving to short-term service issues
  - quality management initiatives
  - ongoing performance measurement
  - updating service level agreements and standards.

Manager's role

The key role in the service delivery process is played by the management team, which is responsible for:

- ◆ Helping to establish the strategy.
- ◆ Understanding the key skills required to deliver outstanding personal and material service.
- ◆ Establishing, monitoring and updating service delivery processes.
- ◆ Coaching employees in personal and material service delivery skills.
- ◆ Acting as an example in delivering outstanding customer service.

We have found that managers play the critical 'make or break' step in the service delivery process.

The rest of this book will concentrate on providing information, skills and tools to be used to establish and maintain effective service delivery processes.

Company profile

British Airways (BA) was one of the first organisations in the UK to successfully implement a service management model, and though it has been discussed often, it is still one of the best examples of making a company profitable directly by changing the customer service approach. Unfortunately, as we can see from current results, the company failed in the long-term to keep in touch with its customers, and once again has to struggle to redefine itself in relation to its business success.

The approach they took initially under Colin Marshall was as follows.

Where were they when they started?

When Colin Marshall took over BA in 1983, the airline had been restructured and the workforce had been reduced from over 60,000 to approximately 37,000. He decided he wanted to differentiate BA in terms of the quality of the service provided – he wanted BA to be the best airline in the world.

BA conducted extensive market research so that they were able to clearly measure their starting point, before any new customer service strategies were implemented. This customer research also gave some clear indicators of potential areas for improvement. For instance, in the normal run of events the customer research indicated that BA did a good job. However, the four factors of highest value were defined as:

♦ Care and concern on the part of public contact personnel.
♦ Adaptability of policies and procedures.
♦ Recovery – the ability to correct things that had gone wrong.
♦ Problem-solving capability of the front-line personnel.

The research revealed that when problems occurred, the airline did not do a good job in handling them. As a result, only 50 per cent of customers said they would fly again after a problem had occurred. This clearly indicated a need to provide *skills and process review checks* when problems occurred.

Strategy

Historically the British often confuse the words service and servitude! The airline had a reputation for being efficient but standoffish. Colin Marshall initiated a strategy that he named Putting the Customer First. While most organisations use a slogan, without the commitment behind it, it is almost impossible to make it succeed. Colin Marshall did the opposite, making sure he implemented all the steps in the service management model (see page 21). Having heard about SAS, and the success of its approach, he ensured BA emulated this methodology.

To communicate the strategy clearly to all employees his team designed a clear identity for the campaign, issued a quarterly Putting the Customer First newsletter and supported it with posters, buttons and banners. In addition, he talked internally to employees about the strategy at every opportunity. Please note that he did not communicate externally about the initiative until after several other steps had been taken.

People

Within a two-year time frame, BA conducted 'wall-to-wall training', i.e. awareness-building seminars for all employees. The programme was called Putting People First and was presented in large group sessions (180 people) by Time Manager International, the organisation that had helped Jan Carlzon at SAS. Each group was made up of employees from different areas of the company such as baggage handling, sales and reservations, flight crew, cabin crew, etc. The content of the programmes was originally called Personal Service through Personal Development and was based on the premise that if employees feel better about themselves, they will be better able to give personalised service.

These sessions provided a unique opportunity for the employees from different areas to get to know each other and reduce some of the departmental barriers between them. In addition, the sessions ensured that the whole company heard and understood the customer service message.

Processes

Alongside the strategy and the training, BA also changed and upgraded many of its service delivery processes. They changed the corporate identity to fit in with the airline's new image.

Continuous improvement

As a result of the Putting People First events, over 100 Customer First teams were established. These teams were made up of volunteers from many functional groups (baggage handlers, reservations, etc) and each team was created to improve a specific factor to help deliver exceptional customer service. At any one time, as many as 1,000 of the airline's staff were involved in one of these teams.

Market research remains a perpetual and routine process, used to feed back more data to Customer First teams and to management. The teams made recommendations and, as a result, many new services and programmes were developed and offered to customers, such as better systems for minors travelling alone, and better retrieval of lost and found items.

After the initial Putting People First programme was completed, BA implemented a further culture change initiative called A Day in the Life where all staff could experience many of the functional areas involved in running a business. Each department – baggage handling, flight crew, sales and reservations, etc – established an interactive display. The groups of 180 divided into smaller groups and moved from one department to another experiencing A Day in the Life of the airline. At the end of the day they would complete a case study and compete with other groups to see who could run the airline the most successfully. Programmes such as these helped to reinforce the ongoing importance of internal service as a way of delivering exceptional external customer service.

Management/leadership

All members of BA's executive team supported the Customer First strategy.

- Colin Marshall personally opened over 60 per cent of the more than 200 Putting People First Programmes that were run.
- All the executive team participated in the programmes.
- A specific programme was designed for management called Managing People First, to provide managers with the skills they needed to coach and reinforce the customer service techniques on an ongoing basis.

The implementation of this service model produced the following results:

- BA was voted airline of the year several years in a row.
- Word spread rapidly about the change in service and BA was cited in many books, producing great PR for the company.
- BA's commitment to the approach proved that a large organisation can improve its service delivery, but only if it institutes all facets of the service management model, and continues this process for at least two years.
- BA became the benchmark upon which many other companies based their strategies. They have been repeatedly quoted and set as an example in numerous articles and books in both the UK and the US.

Exercise	Assess your current performance against the model. Answer each question with a number from one to ten as follows:

                          1 = poor performance in this area
                          5 = average performance
                          10 = exceptional performance.

Strategy

1. To what extent is your customer service strategy clear?
2. To what extent is your customer service slogan repeated by all?
3. To what extent have you defined your customer service values?
4. To what extent have you communicated your customer service strategy?

Overall rating:

People

1. To what extent have you defined the job requirements for service providers?
2. To what extent do you train your people in personal service skills?
3. To what extent do you measure personal service standards?
4. To what extent do you reward exceptional personal service?

Overall rating:

Processes

1. To what extent have you defined your material service processes?
2. To what extent do you measure your current performance?
3. To what extent do you define internal service interactions?
4. To what extent have you established service level agreements?

Overall rating

Continuous improvement

1. To what extent have you made it easy for customers to complain?
2. To what extent do you train people to handle complaints?

3. How effective are you at solving the problem as it happens?
4. How effective are you in looking for the root cause and changing processes as a result of customer complaints?

Overall rating:

Managers

1. To what extent are your managers directing the team rather than leading?
2. To what extent do your managers see customer service as part of their job?
3. To what extent do managers coach their staff on personal service skills?
4. To what extent do managers interact with customers?

Overall rating:

How did your team rate? Which area do you think needs the most work? Depending on the results of this assessment, you may choose to review Chapters 3 to 10 in terms of your priorities rather than follow the sequence of this book.

Chapter 3:   Strategy
Chapter 4:   People, hiring
Chapter 5:   People, personal service skills
Chapter 6:   People, managing the customer interaction
Chapter 7:   Processes, setting standards and service level agreements
Chapter 8:   Processes, dealing with customer complaints
Chapter 9:   Continuous improvement processes
Chapter 10: Management/leadership, coaching and motivating employees.

Where are you now?

Before an organisation can begin a customer service improvement strategy (unless it's a new company with no history), it's important to identify the current standards in terms of strategy, personal and material service and continuous improvement.

The benefits of defining where you are now include:

◆ Having a clear starting point in your customer service improvement campaign.

- Being able to measure progress as you institute different approaches.
- Benchmarking your group/function with other similar organisations and groups.
- Gathering more specific data about what the customer actually wants from your company/product/service.

There are several ways to assess the current levels of customer service you are providing (see Figure 3).

- customer service questionnaires
- telephone interviews with customers
- focus groups
- face-to-face interviews
- on-line research.

Companies can choose to conduct the research themselves, which has several advantages and disadvantages:

Advantages:

- The company has complete access to all data.
- It provides an opportunity to build customer relationships.

Disadvantages:

- Designing market research requires specialised expertise.
- Conducting market research is time-consuming.
- There will not be a neutral perspective.

Conversely, using outside companies can have several advantages and disadvantages:

Advantages:

- The company gets a neutral third-party perspective.
- It is less time-consuming for the company.
- An outside provider has existing expertise in designing survey instruments.

Disadvantages:

- The consulting organisation may not completely understand your product/service and the information you require.
- You lose the opportunity to communicate directly with your customers.

Type of Research	Characteristics	To consider
Customer service surveys/ questionnaires	• Sent to small groups of customers • Customers are selected on demographic data, buying patterns, geographical area, etc • Easily summarised • Normally quantitative data	• There may not be much opportunity to receive individual comments • Many customers can be surveyed • Response rate can be low: fewer than 5 per cent of customers may complete the survey
Telephone interviews	• A structured questionnaire is normally prepared • Customers are selected using specific criteria, as with written surveys • Data is summarised	• The benefits of this approach are that there is more opportunity to collect individual remarks • Can be time-consuming • Fewer people can be interviewed
Focus groups	• Customers are selected according to pre-screening criteria • Groups of customers are interviewed together using a structured questionnaire	• Rich qualitative feedback • Fewer people can be interviewed • Time-consuming
Face-to-face interviews	• Again, the information required for market research is decided • Individuals conducting the research meet customers one-on-one, either in a prepared interview, or at the place where the service is provided	• Rich qualitative feedback • Time-consuming • Can be hard to ensure the people meet the profile you are looking for
On-line research	• Web-based community sites are beginning to offer corporate services to conduct on-line research • Specific groups are targeted, and the time for the on-line research is publicised by the client and the community site provider • On-line mediators facilitate the session	• Very cost-effective • Less time-consuming than face-to-face interviews • Good qualitative research • Complete transcripts are then available • Can be used by the service company to build customer loyalty

Fig. 3   Research checklist.

Companies that can help you conduct customer research include market research organisations, independent consulting firms, firms that focus on specific market segments (eg Datapro in technical support centre environments) and many new web community site providers such as Talk City.

Specific examples of the differing forms of market research are:

- Customer service questionnaires:
  - to customers to evaluate their service experience, such as Datapro.
  - conducting internal attitude surveys to assess employee satisfaction.
  - using customer feedback forms.
- Telephone interviews with customers, such as a garage calling after a car has been serviced. This could be internally or externally implemented.
- Focus groups: companies using brainstorming sessions with customers to evaluate new product ideas.
- Face-to-face research:
  - talking to new employees who might have a fresh outlook.
  - using secret shopper services (for retail environments).
- On-line research: facilitating a chat about specific products.

Exercise

Decide your approach to conducting customer research. Think about the different ways of surveying customers that we have discussed:

- customer service questionnaires
- telephone interviews
- focus groups
- face-to-face interviews
- on-line research.

1. Which approach will you use to discover where are you now?
2. Which approach do you think would gather the most useful data?
3. To what extent will you conduct the research using your staff?
4. What outside providers could provide additional service to you?

Service cycle

The detailed assessment of where you are now can start by understanding your cycle of service for meeting customer needs. What this means is to track examples of your customers' interaction with your company when using its products and services. For instance, if you operate a consulting company, the steps in the service cycle might be as follows:

- Stimulate leads by placing advertisements in journals (material service).
- Design a web page to raise interest (material service).
- Customer calls (material and personal service).
- Customer talks to consultant on the phone (personal service).
- Customer meets consultant (personal service).
- Customer books work and consultant performs said duties (personal service).
- Consultant invoices client (material service).
- Client pays bill (material service).
- Consultant follows up with client to check on quality of service (personal service).
- Consultant sends client regular newsletters (material service).

For each step in this service cycle it is important to assess:

1. How easy is it for the customer to work with us?
2. What could be done to make our systems more customer-friendly?
3. What else could we do to make our service experience more positive?

Hotel assessment

Following is a sample checklist for a hotel to evaluate where it stands in providing exceptional personal and material service. Evaluating the effectiveness of strategy and management requires a general approach. Assessing material and personal service standards usually follows the service cycle. For instance, for the hotel it would start with the booking systems, move to check-in, etc.

Strategy

- Is there a visible customer service mission statement?
- Is there a visible customer service 'slogan'?
- Is the General Manager's name available to guests – or is 'the management' the typical signature of the day?
- Is there a personal letter from the General Manager greeting each guest?
- Is there a formal process for gathering feedback?
- Is any formal customer research done?

Note: if none of the above exists, it's a good indication that service is not a real priority.

Material service checklist

Lobby/check-in:
- Is there a concierge?
- Is there a doorman?
- Is a map of the facility given at check-in?

Bedroom (though most business travellers travel alone, more and more are taking their spouses along, but most business rooms are only designed for one person):
- Is the TV large enough?
- Is there space to walk around the room with two people in it?
- Are the explanations for phone usage clear?
- If there are quick dial buttons on the telephone, do they work?
- Is there a voicemail and if so can you access it from the telephone or do you have to go through the operator?
- Is there a phone jack for an Internet connection?
- Is there a table to work on?
- Is the height of the table comfortable to work on?
- Is the lighting sufficient?
- Is the storage space sufficient for two people?
- Is the bed comfortable?
- Is there a clock radio and does it work?
- Are there two chairs to sit on?

Bathroom
- Can two people be in the bathroom at the same time?

◆ Is a hairdryer supplied? Is there a convenient plug?
◆ Is there shampoo, conditioner, lotion and mouthwash?
◆ Are there enough towels – at least two per person?
◆ Is there space to lay out toiletries?

Health club:
◆ Are the hours of the health club convenient for business guests?
◆ Are the hours consistently displayed in the hotel information, on the door and given by the hotel staff?
◆ Is the capacity of the health club sufficient for the size of the hotel?
◆ Is there a swimming pool, cardiovascular equipment and weights?
◆ Are there towels, a fan and drinking water?

Personal service checklist

As you can see, the moments of truth for personal service are different from those for material service, but many may originate from poor or inadequate material service standards.

Lobby/check-in:
◆ Does the check-in person smile and use the customer's name?
◆ Is the lobby staff able to answer simple questions about the hotel and facility?
◆ Is a map offered to guide guests around the hotel?
◆ Is the bell staff knowledgeable and willing?

Bedroom:
◆ Are guests shown around the room by the bell staff?
◆ Does the housekeeping staff smile at guests in the hallway?
◆ Does the housekeeping staff greet guests as they are walking in the hallways?

Operator:
◆ Do telephone operators answer the phone with a smile in their voices?
◆ Does the telephone staff use the correct tone of voice?
◆ Is telephone staff helpful in meeting customer needs?

Health club:

◆ Is the staff – if any – willing and helpful?

Dealing with unusual requests:

◆ Does the staff know how to answer requests that are not 'normal'? For instance, when asked if the health club can be opened early, generally 'no' is the common though unnecessary response.
◆ Are these requests tracked to determine if changes need to be made to material service standards in order to meet them? (For instance opening the health club at 8 a.m. is unacceptable to business guests.)

Continuous improvement

◆ Are customer complaints currently tracked?
◆ Is the customer offered recompense if not satisfied?
◆ Are material service problems tracked?
◆ Are processes and procedures constantly reviewed to update standards?

Managers

◆ Do managers take any regular customer service training?
◆ Do managers play the role of the service provider at any time?
◆ Do managers understand the difference between personal and material service?
◆ Do managers coach their staff on a regular basis on providing customer service?

The best way to create a checklist for your organisation is to get someone who understands customer service to:

◆ View the system as a beginner would without knowing anything as an employee – new recruits are great at doing this.
◆ Ask any employees who have friends to try and 'break the system' within the boundaries of fairness.
◆ Ask for formalised research into customer service standards from an external consultant.

Exercise	Define your service cycle and assess current standards of service. What are the main steps in your service delivery cycle? How is the customer introduced to you? What happens next? What are the other important steps?

For each step in this service cycle:
1. How easy is it for the customer to work with you?
2. What could be done to make your systems more customer-friendly?
3. What else could you do to make your service experience more positive?
4. What other services could you add?
5. What processes actually hinder the service delivery at this point?
6. What processes might be added to smooth service delivery at this point?
7. What will you do differently to improve the effectiveness of your service delivery cycle?

Case Study: Cleanworks: the driving force

As we saw in Chapter 1, Cleanworks is a new organisation. Their four core competencies were defined as:

- ◆ top-quality customer service
- ◆ high-quality cleaning results
- ◆ pick-up and delivery
- ◆ management expertise.

When the concept of providing exceptional customer service was originally defined in their charter, the company viewed it as being skills-related. When they started conducting more research, they discovered that to really create a customer service culture meant aligning the differing providers around strategy, defining clear job requirements, instituting a customer service training programme and ensuring effective service delivery processes. How they approached creating a customer service culture will be defined in detail in the following chapters.

Where are they now?

As they are a new company, there is no data to gather in terms of their current status, but instead they did two things.

First they conducted extensive research (described briefly in Chapter 1) to identify customer needs. They used an advertising agency to conduct focus groups with customers. The advertising agency then used this data to begin creating a corporate identity and slogan.

Secondly they mapped the service delivery process from start to finish as a way to anticipate problem areas and design strategies in anticipation of the issues. The key steps in the process were:

- To solicit customer business by advertising, flyers and other promotional efforts.
- The customer calls the service centre to arrange pick-up of laundry/dry cleaning.
- The van driver picks up the laundry and/or dry cleaning.
- The laundry and dry cleaning arrive at the plant and are unloaded.
- The laundry and dry cleaning are returned to the customer.
- The customer receives a bill once a month.

Additional contacts between Cleanworks and the customer anywhere in the service cycle could be:

- Call to obtain answers to technical questions.
- Call to change delivery dates.

Understanding these steps in the service delivery cycle enabled Cleanworks to establish service standards for each of these components. These standards will be listed more fully in Chapter 7.

Case study: Kitchen Barn: the driving force ⎯⎯⎯⎯⎯⎯⎯⎯⎯⎯⎯⎯⎯⎯⎯

Kitchen Barn had hired a new Senior Vice President at the same time that a new retail organisation, with venture capital funding had just entered the marketplace. A new retail organisation had recently been established and the rapid growth of web-based selling was challenging their traditional distribution channels. While the organisation separately decided to investigate more web-based and catalogue marketing, the Senior VP of Retail, Gary, was given the task of deciding strategies to protect Kitchen Barn's position in the retail market. While there are several positioning possibilities, since Kitchen Barn is a premium price provider Gary felt that the most effective direction would be to use the top-service, premium-priced model for the business.

In the later chapters we will present how he drove the strategy, instituted a comprehensive training programme, consistently updated procedures, and used reinforcement to keep the initiative alive and well. His management team, as the main trainers for the programme, acted as the champions for the process and were able to coach and reinforce the skills.

Where are they now?

Kitchen Barn completed regular secret shopper surveys, conducted by an outside agency, to assess their current levels of service. These surveys showed clearly that while the personal service was normally acceptable, customers still perceived the company products to be overpriced. Also there tended to be an inconsistency in the way customers were treated. The research gave valuable foundation data, and was updated as training was rolled out, when more specific focus areas were identified. In addition, Gary would spend time with new employees within four weeks of them joining the organisation, to ask them what they would change based on their prior experience and their insights in their first days of employment.

Case study: Internet Express: the driving force

Before Internet Express was created by the merger of Network Logic and MacDonald Software, Network Logic was uniquely positioned towards a small, highly technical audience. The people who worked for the organisation were highly-qualified engineers whose customers were similar to them: technically competent and passionate about the product.

As a result of the merger, the company's products were repositioned into more of the enterprise server market and the customer base broadened. Now the customer could be anyone, from the technical-development engineer, to the Vice President of Operations to the end user. This meant that the role of the technical support function changed from fixing the problem with a person who was technically literate, to sometimes having to 'fix the customer' in terms of educating and communicating effectively. The customer's agenda could now be anything from needing information, to wanting complex data explained in a simple way, to political manoeuvring.

As a result, the requirements for those who interacted with the customer changed, and individuals needed to become more 'problem managers' rather than 'problem fixers'. Rather than just training the people in personal service skills, the Vice President, Arthur, initiated a complete service development strategy covering the customer services values, changing hiring requirements, instituting service level agreements and changing measurement criteria. More details will be included in later chapters.

Where are they now?

Internet Express commissioned a preliminary written customer service survey in order to assess current customer satisfaction levels. This survey indicated that apart from the considerable product issues (such as that the product was unreliable, product upgrades took too long), the staff were perceived as discourteous and unprofessional. This survey provided the base knowledge for the customer service improvement process. In addition, the company initiated a programme, conducted by managers, to call a small percentage of customers within two days of them interacting with the support centre. The purpose of these calls was, first for managers to discover the customer's direct perception of the service received, and secondly an opportunity to build customer relationships. The customers selected would normally be from major companies, with whom Internet Express wanted to have a long-term business partnership. The data gathered, although less than the more formal written survey, provided a more in-depth qualitative perspective of the customer's needs. _____

Discussion points

1. How clear is your customer service strategy? Is it visible, communicated consistently to all, and practised by senior management? Remember that any message gets diluted 50 per cent at each passing, what can you do to communicate the strategy, and the commitment to the strategy, to your entire organisation?

2. To what extent are the people you are hiring customer focused? How do you reward them for providing exceptional personal service? How do you train them in customer service skills?

3. To what extent are your material service standards defined? How effective are your service delivery processes?

4. How do you track any problems that arise? How are the solutions to short-term problems incorporated into long-term process improvement?

5. To what extent do managers 'walk the talk' in delivering exceptional service? How far do they coach employees to deliver exceptional service?

6. To what extent have you conducted, or are you conducting, customer research? Which of the approaches described in this chapter would provide you with the most relevant feedback on your current service levels and customer requirements? What

could you do to institute a more formalised customer research policy?

7. When you evaluated the components of the service management model: strategy, people, process, continuous improvements and management, which required the most immediate action? Which appeared to be pretty successful?

Summary

- The service management model is the methodology used to institute a customer service culture within an organisation, rather than using customer service as a slogan or platitude with no cohesive strategy.

- Organisations that have adopted this comprehensive service management approach have succeeded in becoming market leaders in their field, eg Ritz Carlton (see later).

- Before beginning the service improvement initiatives, it is important to assess where you are now in terms of your current service delivery. There are two main ways that this can be accomplished, and they can be used together: one can be externally customer-focused and the other can be internally, more systems-focused.

- The first approach is to use professional market research to find out your current standing with your customers. This can be done both internally using telephone questionnaires, focus groups, etc and externally using consultants and research service companies.

- The second way is to map your service delivery cycle, in order to define the important steps involved in meeting your customers' needs, and then evaluate what could be done to improve the process at each point.

- Once you have evaluated your current competence, you can decide which components of the service management model you wish to address in what sequence, in order to implement a customer-focused culture.

Without clear management commitment, customer service will not improve

CHAPTER 3

Customer Service Strategy

As we discussed in the last chapter, changing or instituting a customer service culture requires not only senior management commitment, but also a clear and cohesive customer service strategy. In this chapter we will explain and discuss the important steps needed to create this cohesive customer service direction. These steps include creating a customer service vision and strategy, assessing the critical competencies and weaknesses in delivering exceptional service as they relate to the customer needs identified in Chapter 2 and by defining customer service values. We also need to ensure that the company, team or group remains focused on an ongoing basis on exceeding customer expectations using customer service as a key result area. Finally we will create a plan to communicate this strategy clearly and consistently to all employees.

Strategic planning

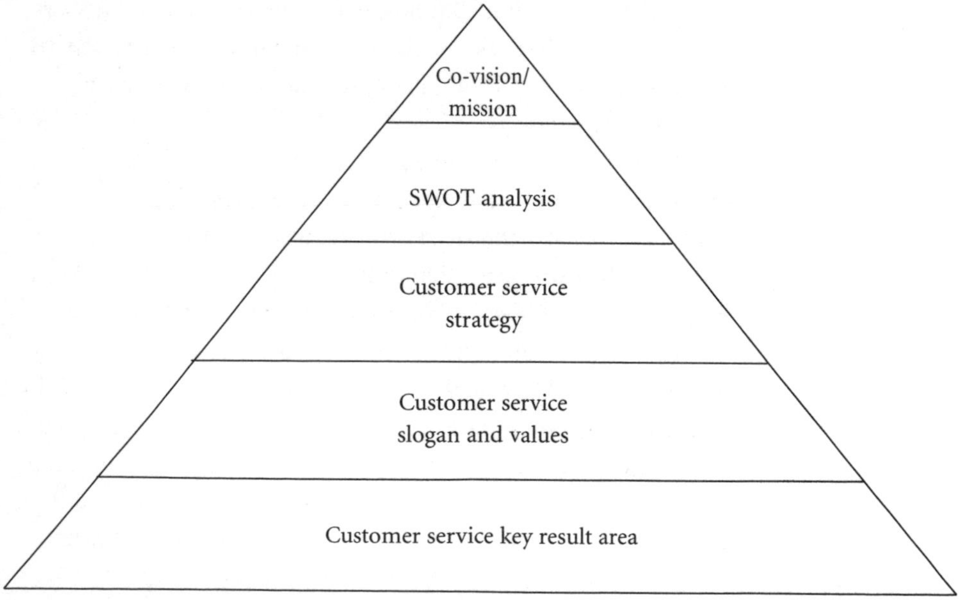

Fig. 4. Strategic planning pyramid.

The company vision statement

The company's *vision statement* gives a clear image of where the company wants to be in the future, including the reason for its existence. The vision statement is intended to be inspirational and to act as a general direction for the organisation. It serves as the guiding philosophy for the organisation and helps to define the way the company operates, focusing attention on the future.

Questions asked when companies are defining their vision statements include:

♦ What is the company's ultimate purpose?
♦ What do you want the company to look like in the future?
♦ What does the company want to be?
♦ What is the company's ultimate theme or image?
♦ What is the company's ultimate contribution to the customer?

The purpose of a company's vision statement is to guide daily decision-making in the organisation and capture the essence of what needs to be done in order to succeed.

Examples of vision statements are:

♦ **Oracle:** To enable the information age through network computing.
♦ **Kepner Tregoe:** We focus on the human side of change through providing skills development programmes and consulting services.
♦ **Raychem:** To win the respect of our customers around the world, by being a leader in delivering innovative solutions.
♦ **Ritz Carlton Hotels:** The Ritz Carlton is a place where the genuine care and comfort of our guests is our highest mission.

> The statement captures the essence of the business direction and can act as an inspiration for future performance.

When a customer service strategy is initiated, it's important that it is in alignment with the organisation's overall direction as stated in the company vision. For instance, a real estate company created a vision statement saying that it wanted to be the market leader in property management services with an emphasis on customer service. However they also were planning to cut costs and negotiate higher rents with tenants. There were two strategies contributing to this vision. The first was improving customer service, the second related to changing their cost structure to increase profits. The two strategies were at odds with each other and therefore the company made the decision to drop the customer service focus and instead use greater profitability to achieve their vision.

The Company mission statement

The company's *mission statement* communicates the vision by considering several critical factors:

◆ What does the company want to do?
◆ Who is the company's customer?
◆ What are the company's values?
◆ What profit is needed?

An effective mission statement must:

◆ be clear and understandable to everyone in the company
◆ be brief enough to be remembered
◆ clearly specify the company's business
◆ be based on and reflective of the overall vision of the company
◆ reflect the inherent skills of the company
◆ be broad enough to allow flexibility, but not so broad as to lose focus
◆ be able to serve as a template by which decisions are made
◆ reflect the values, beliefs, philosophies and culture of the company
◆ include a commitment to the economic motives of the company.

Raychem's mission statement for 1998 was to:

◆ sell $75 million in new products
◆ increase market share from 15 to 17 per cent in a specific product range
◆ create new business opportunities.

> The mission statement is more specific than the vision statement and can act as a general direction upon which to build the beliefs and actions that will create a customer service culture.

SWOT analysis

Focusing on customer service, *SWOT analysis* takes a probing look at the Strengths, Weaknesses, Opportunities and Threats that face the company or team in delivering exceptional service. The analysis is a process of investigating and brainstorming the factors working for and against the company that could affect overall service levels. *Strengths* and *weaknesses* refer to the company's internal advantages and potential disadvantages. It is important that these factors are in the direct control of the team carrying out the analysis. *Opportunities* and *threats* allude to aspects outside the company's direct control that might open up potential (opportunities) or result in negative consequences (threats). Opportunities and threats can originate from outside the company in the market at large, from other organisations, or even from other departments within the company itself.

> The purpose of SWOT analysis is to view the world in which you are trying to provide service from the vantage point of the big picture.

This ensures that the planned strategy and direction are possible, given the company's inherent strengths and weaknesses. It also ensures that the strategy is geared towards capitalising on opportunities and minimising threats.

As an example, the results of a SWOT analysis undertaken by a training and development consulting firm are as follows.

Strengths

- 20 years' experience
- excellent network of contacts
- specialised functional expertise in Situational Leadership™ and Break-It Thinking™
- great marketing skills
- package of programmes available to sell
- organised.

Weaknesses

+ lack of administrative support
+ lack of procedures
+ limited financial resources
+ too many customised programmes
+ inadequate resource of trainers.

Opportunities

+ thriving market
+ companies are downsizing, creating more demand for contract trainers
+ more companies are outsourcing trainers
+ many business publications write about the importance of developing human potential as critical to an organisation's success.

Threats

+ Growth in alternative training delivery methods such as computer-based training may reduce the demand for 'classroom' training
+ there are many one-person consulting firms
+ future financial market stability
+ difficulty in raising market awareness
+ changing company strategies and people moving from one company to another.

Exercise   Conduct a SWOT analysis for your company for delivering exceptional service. You may want to revisit the exercises you completed in Chapter 2 on defining your service cycle and ways it can be improved.

1. What are your company's strengths?
2. What are your company's weaknesses?
3. What are your company's opportunities?
4. What are your company's threats?

Customer service strategy

Customer service strategy comes from the company's vision, mission and SWOT analysis. For example, Colin Marshall said he wanted British Airways to be the best airline in the world. From this the organisation created its customer service strategy which should capture the essence of what you want the service experience to be for your customers, employees, managers and business associates. It's the vision you want them to have when they think of your customer service.

> A customer service strategy should be inspirational and act as a general direction for the company.

An effective customer service strategy should meet these requirements:
1. It should be developed by the staff.
2. It should be in an easily remembered form.
3. It should set high standards so that accomplishing the strategy means you will be delivering exceptional service.
4. It must have broad support. The entire company – management, staff and supporting activities must 'walk the talk' every day.
5. It must be aligned with the company's vision statement.

The purpose of the customer service strategy is to guide daily decision-making and capture the essence of what customer service needs to be in order to succeed. Examples:
- Avis Rent-A-Car: We're number two, so we try harder.
- Stew Leonard Groceries: Rule 1: The customer is always right. Rule 2: If you think the customer is wrong, read Rule 1.

Customer service slogan

The *customer service slogan* or *'mantra'* exists to capture the substance of the customer service strategy in a short phrase.

> The benefit of the slogan is to focus energy and interest around the customer service strategy.

Examples include:

◆ Nike: Just do it.
◆ Amdahl: A customer problem is an Amdahl problem.
◆ British Airways: Put the customer first.
◆ Ford: Quality is job one.

Too often organisations create a slogan, but then don't follow through in other areas to manage the service delivery process. As a result, the slogan has the opposite of the desired effect, resulting in increased frustration from both internal and external customers. The most obvious outcome from establishing a slogan is an internal marketing communications campaign that is written off as 'management's flavour of the month'.

The president of a financial printing company decreed that customer service was a priority for 1998, without understanding how difficult it would be to make his vision a reality. His team, with unclear direction and no senior management commitment, proceeded to undertake a company-wide communication programme, complete with gizmos (cups, T-shirts, etc). The result, as you might have expected, was extra costs, a 'muddy' message and no difference in customer service levels.

The Ritz Carlton hotel chain has named its customer service philosophy The Gold Standard. It includes:

The Credo:

◆ We pledge to provide the finest personal service and facilities for our guests who will always enjoy a warm, relaxed yet fine ambience.
◆ The Ritz Carlton experience enlivens the senses, instils well-being and fulfils even the unexpressed wishes of our guests.

Slogan:

◆ We are ladies and gentlemen serving ladies and gentlemen.

Three Steps of Service:

1. A warm, sincere greeting. Use the guest name, if and when possible.
2. Anticipation and compliance with guest needs.
3. A fond farewell. Give them a warm goodbye and use their names, if and when possible.

The Twenty Basics:
Twenty rules for ensuring excellent service.

Exercise	1. Write down your company's vision.
	2. Write down your company's mission statement.
	3. Write down your company's customer service strategy.
	4. Write down your company's customer service slogan.

Think about the following questions with regards to your customer service strategy:

♦ Is customer service mentioned in your company's vision and mission statements?

♦ Is anything written in the vision or mission statements that might inhibit delivery of exceptional customer service such as cost management, etc?

♦ Do you have a customer service strategy?

♦ Is senior management committed to the customer service strategy?

♦ Is there a customer service slogan?

♦ Does this slogan have the support and understanding of all people in the company?

♦ If front-line employees were to be asked, would they be able to repeat this slogan and strategy?

If the answer to many of these questions is no, and your SWOT analysis indicated a different business direction, your chances of instituting a successful customer service culture are relatively small. Your challenge is then to decide:

1. Can you obtain senior management commitment and focus?

2. Do you want to continue to build customer service from the bottom up, almost against the culture of the company?

When organisations decide to institute a customer service culture, more often than not they have to slow down in the short term in order to gain management commitment and produce more effective long-term results.

Defining our customer service values

When trying to improve performance, whether it is in customer service, quality, or profitability, there are two elements that need to be addressed: *the task* and *the group process*. The task element relates to anything that needs to be done to achieve the goal and tends to focus on the outcome. The group process element relates to how well people are interacting with each other to produce the desired results. Both components need to be working well in order to meet objectives. For instance, it is hard to deliver great service if two internal departments are squabbling with each other: the group process is not working effectively.

It is also hard to meet customer needs if someone doesn't know what they are supposed to be doing (task element).

The customer service strategy and slogan give direction in terms of what the company wants to achieve: the task element in delivering exceptional customer service. It is equally important for companies to establish customer service values. Defining these values is a way of establishing how people in the company are committed to treating each other: the group process element. These values provide the underlying framework for internal customer service. Ultimately these internal values have a direct impact on external customer service levels.

Values

In building an understanding of customer service values it is critical to establish *the culture of the company*. It also acts as a starting point for developing service level agreements (described in detail in Chapter 7). Material service standards will not be effective if they go against the company's fundamental value system.

Examples of values are:

- achievement
- communication
- customer comes first
- empowerment
- equality
- forgiveness
- honesty
- loyalty
- participation
- respect
- commitment
- cooperation
- empathy
- encouragement
- expertise
- friendship
- innovation/creativity
- open-mindedness
- proactiveness and reactiveness
- responsiveness

◆ sense of humour   ◆ service

◆ sharing the load   ◆ unity

Exercise   Define customer service values:

1. Select a team made up of individuals from different levels in the company.
2. Individually, consider the values you believe are important to your company in delivering exceptional service. The values may be included on the above list, but they may also be different.
3. As a group, combine the values and agree on the top five you believe will contribute to exceeding customer expectations.

Customer service as a key result area

Once a company has committed to instituting a customer service culture, this strategy needs to be included as a fundamental focus for the business, this is called a *key result area*.

What are key result areas?

Key result areas are a tool that categorises the company's *entire* workload. While many organisations set objectives for their members, often there is no direct link between the purpose/mission, the customer service strategy, project milestones and the tasks the individuals have to complete on a day-to-day basis.

> Establishing key result areas is a valuable technique that links the overall priorities and workload of the company with project goals and milestones.

Key result areas do not describe the type of results to be achieved, but rather categorise work into headings. This grouping procedure is a valuable tool in categorising workload as the process complements the way the human brain naturally works.

Building an overview in the brain

Our brains are structured into three levels of consciousness:

- The subconscious brain works 24-hours a day and has, as far as we know, unlimited capacity. The challenge with the subconscious brain is that it runs as a random access device – in other words, it has no filing system from which we can easily call up information.
- We also have a conscious brain, which works only when we are awake and can concentrate on only one thought at a time. As a result, when we have a multitude of tasks to complete we feel overloaded. However, the third level of the brain, the preconscious, helps us by keeping track of an effective overview.
- The preconscious brain can keep an outline of seven +/– two (i.e. five to nine categories). If the group can create a list of approximately seven areas of responsibility covering all aspects of their work, they will have a complete overview from which to set realistic goals and milestones. In addition, employees feel more in control and stress levels are reduced when they can see the big picture.

Organisational key result areas

Examples of typical key result areas are:

1. Financial management/control: most companies have to meet budget requirements, control costs and make a profit.
2. Marketing/sales: most companies have to market their services if they are to survive.
3. Operations: most companies have an operations/process key result area to cover administrative and routine activities.
4. People: most companies have a key result area that captures the essence of their people strategy, including hiring, training and keeping key people.
5. Customer service: having customer service as a key result area for the business ensures that there is organisational focus in this area.
6. Manufacturing and distribution: companies that distribute tangible products often have a manufacturing/distribution key result area.
7. Research and development: to remain current in today's

dynamic environment it's important to allocate time and energy to research and development.

Exercise	Define your team/company's key result areas:

1. Conduct this exercise with multiple members from your management team.
2. Individually, on separate stick-on notes, list the specific tasks that you complete on a regular basis: one task per note. Make sure you list as many activities as you can.
3. If you have categories such as e-mail or telephone, be more specific about the purpose of the e-mail: eg are they to customers, to internal departments, etc.
4. When you are individually running out of ideas, start to work in groups of three.
5. As you work together, eliminate the duplicate tasks or activities.
6. Next, group these tasks or activities under sample headings, such as the ones discussed earlier, or choose from the list below.
7. Make sure you use no more than seven headings.
8. Make sure customer service is one of these headings or key result areas.

List your company's *key result areas*. Some sample categories are shown to help you get started with your own.

Financial	Sales
Marketing	Team development
Customer service	Operations
Communication	Reporting
Projects	Quality
Research and development	Manufacturing
Vendor management	Purchasing
Process improvement	Problem identification

Is customer service a key result area for your business? If it isn't, it is highly unlikely that you will be able to deliver exceptional service. If it is – great news – move on to the next step! If not, ask again if customer service is really a driving force for your business. If it isn't, don't try to begin a customer service campaign. If you're not committed to it, it will not succeed.

Communicating the strategy

Once an organisation has committed to instituting a customer service culture, this strategy and direction needs to be communicated to the entire company. There is only one guideline when trying to announce the strategy: it is communicate, communicate, communicate and then, if in doubt, communicate! You need to balance face-to-face, written and electronic communication channels.

Communication tools and methodologies include:

◆ Regular newsletters around the theme of the customer service initiative.

◆ Design of corporate identity around the customer service strategy, so every communication piece has the same look and feel.

◆ 'Town hall' meetings, where the President/CEO holds regular meetings with the company, restating the customer service theme. With today's technology, even global companies can hold these meetings for all locations using video conferencing and satellite links.

◆ Posters using the slogan.

◆ Badges, T-shirts, sweat shirts, etc.

◆ Training programmes and seminars (see Chapter 5).

◆ E-mail announcements.

◆ Voicemail announcements.

◆ Other give-aways such as desk gizmos, pens, paper cutters, etc.

◆ Contests and awards (see Chapter 10 for more information).

For instance Ritz Carlton introduces all new recruits to its Gold Standard programme in an intensive orientation programme. All 14,000 ladies and gentlemen keep this information in sight and in mind using a pocket-sized laminated card. Research with organisations such as Ritz Carlton has shown that it takes approximately two years until this message is received, understood, believed and acted upon within an entire organisation.

Case study: Cleanworks: defining strategy _____

Cleanworks decided to hold a planning session with key players to clearly articulate the service strategy. The meeting included not only employees of the company, but the key suppliers who were helping to make the Cleanworks vision a reality.

Cleanworks' vision

Initially the group brainstormed lots of ideas to try to capture what would make Cleanworks unique, some of which are listed below:

◆ time-saving
◆ keeps your life clean
◆ gives you back time
◆ done the way you want

◆ liberating
◆ unprecedented
◆ revolutionary

Remembering that a vision is not the same as a slogan, and that it should help to guide what a company wants to be when it grows up, Cleanworks finally defined its vision statement as: 'Cleanworks will be the preferred cleaning provider for the year 2000 and beyond'.

When this vision was compared with a customer service direction, the two approaches were found to be in sync. Customer service would be a key strategy in making sure Cleanworks was the preferred cleaning provider, and customer service, as we discussed in Chapter 1, is a key aspect to facilitate long-term business growth.

Cleanworks' mission statement

As the company is in its early development, the decision was made to formalise a mission statement after it had built its first plant. The mission statement, as we discussed, is far more concrete and tangible than the vision, and therefore requires real data in order to make it feasible.

Cleanworks' SWOT analysis

Cleanworks' version of a SWOT analysis was made up of market research data: it focused on the opportunities and threats in the market as a whole.

As we discussed briefly in Chapter 2, opportunities identified were:

◆ no one player in the market
◆ lots of corner shops, with limited resources
◆ more organisations in the industry, because of size, were limited in both ability to advertise and in achieving economies of scale

- people were gravitating towards services that made their lives easier because of time pressures
- customer service in the industry was notoriously bad with many documented complaints
- customers indicated they would be willing to pay a premium for top-quality material and personal service.

Possible threats discussed were:
- recruiting people with a positive customer service attitude in such traditionally low-paying jobs
- running a completely new business
- possible future competition
- instituting home delivery.

The company created a comprehensive business plan that it used to clarify the investment and cost of return, which proved that, despite the potential threats, this was still a long-term viable business proposition. Furthermore, customer service remained a key element in this elaborate business strategy.

Cleanworks' strategy and slogan

For this business, the slogan was easier to articulate than the vision statement! The slogan decided on was: 'We care for your laundry so that you can get on with your life'.

Cleanworks' values

The group identified the key values it thought were essential to smooth the group process. They used the letters of the company name for the values:

C   **C**ommitment to the company and each other
L   **L**isten with the intent to understand
E   **E**mpathy: putting ourselves in our customers' shoes
A   **A**ttitude: the customer is king/queen
N   **N***ever* say no to the customer
W   **W**ork together to meet customer needs
O   **O**pen-ended questions to ensure we are identifying needs
R   **R**esponsiveness to customer requests
K   **K**nowledge in our field
S   **S**ense of humour.

Customer service as a key result area

Cleanworks defined its key result areas as follows:

1.   Customer service.
2.   Marketing.
3.   Call centre.
4.   Dry cleaning/laundry.
5.   Delivery.
6.   People.
7.   Financial control.

   In the business plan, customer service is and has always been a fundamental part of how they add value to the company.

Communicating the Cleanworks strategy

As Cleanworks currently didn't exist, the decision was made to use the slogan and vision in the recruitment campaign. In this way, applicants knew that a customer service mentality and skills were required. After the employees were hired, communication became a mixture of the training programmes (see Chapter 5) and the rewards and recognition systems (see Chapter 10). Communicating the strategy is far easier with a new company than an existing one, as you can see from the other case studies.

Case study: Kitchen Barn: setting the strategy – the vision and mission

The core of Kitchen Barn is expressed in their vision: 'We are in the business of enhancing the quality of life at home – helping people derive greater pleasure and social enjoyment from their home environment through high-quality, well-designed innovative products and exemplary service.'

   As you can see, customer service is inherently part of this value proposition.

   Kitchen Barn's mission statement was: 'To become the dominant home-centred speciality retailer for quality and design conscious consumers in the US by the year 2000.

◆   #1 share of the market in each category in which we participate
◆   preferred choice by customers
◆   15 per cent annual sales growth
◆   10 per cent pre-tax profit.'

   When Gary's drive to improve customer service was compared with these statements and the history of the business, they were found to be in very close alignment. Many of the most successful retail organisations have created their market niche using customer service as the way they differentiate themselves from their competitors.

Kitchen Barn SWOT Analysis

A strategic planning process with the executive team identified the following sample strengths, weaknesses, opportunities and threats as they related specifically to providing exceptional service.

Strengths:
- passion
- humour
- improvisation
- compassion
- commitment
- talent
- organisation
- reputation

Weaknesses:
- underuse
- systems reactive not proactive
- non-cohesive direction
- lack of vision/optimism
- unfocused
- lack of punctuality
- no planning
- no follow-up

Opportunities:
- services (interior design)
- direct mail
- involvement in community
- editorial
- new suppliers
- new markets
- advertising
- Internet
- promotions/city events
- trends
- creating own product
- baby boomers

Threats:
- competition
- bad press
- economy
- disloyalty
- managing supply chain
- market saturation
- vendors
- lack of integrity

Despite what appeared to be a clear vision and mission statement, the customer service message did not appear to be understood on the shop floor. This confused the executive team who thought this was understood by all working for Kitchen Barn. As a result, they realised that the customer service focus would benefit from a slogan and clearer communication with the people on the front line.

Creating a customer service strategy

Gary decided to restate the importance of customer service to Kitchen Barn by saying the strategy was: 'To provide the best customer service in the housewares industry in order to maximise customer satisfaction and retention.'

Creating a customer service slogan

From this high-level strategy statement, the slogan for Kitchen Barn became: 'To make every customer feel like an honoured *GUEST* in our stores'.

The combination of the strategy statement and the slogan would act as the foundation for the rest of the service management programme.

Customer service values

The team of district managers completed the values exercise in this chapter to clarify the customer service values for the retail organisation. When the results were collated, it showed that the team had agreed upon a cohesive set of values:

◆ respect
◆ honesty
◆ sense of humour
◆ creativity
◆ commitment.

Customer service as a key result area
Kitchen Barn defined its key result areas as follows:

1. Customer service.
2. Marketing.
3. Sales.
4. Merchandising.
5. Inventory management.
6. Operations.
7. People/morale.
8. Financial management.

Under the customer service key result area, the team highlighted possible programmes such as:

◆ creating a clientele book system
◆ special orders

- problem-solving
- personal shopping
- additional services: registry, wrapping
- standards
- philosophy.

More specific tasks and activities to support this strategy and formalise these ideas will be described in later chapters.

Communicating the customer service strategy

As the SWOT analysis had revealed, all associates did not have a clear understanding of the customer service strategy. Gary refocused his communications around customer service in the following way:

- He sent out a letter to all staff describing the strategy and slogan and explaining the reason for this direction.
- He went to every store during the pre-Christmas roll-out to personally communicate with as many staff members as possible the importance of customer service.
- He initiated and supported a 'wall-to-wall' training programme (see Chapter 5).
- He produced a logo for the GUEST approach.
- His retail operations team created a monthly GUEST update newsletter.
- He started special rewards and recognition programmes to support the strategy (see Chapter 10).
- He initiated a weekly conference call with all 20 district managers, where the first agenda item was customer service: sharing success stories and ideas for improvement.
- Not only did he communicate within his division, but with the rest of the organisation about the customer service focus.

Case study: Internet Express: setting the strategy

Arthur decided to hold several off-site meetings with his direct and extended management team to set a cohesive customer service strategy. His approach was hard to implement consistently because of the overall vision and culture of the company.

Internet Express vision and mission

Internet Express had a combined vision and mission that had guided the strategic direction of the organisation in the five years of its existence and differing company names. This statement was: 'To be the world-wide leader in enterprise software for distributed-computing enterprise environments'.

Obviously customer service plays an important role in becoming a world-wide leader in any specific field. However, in the software industry having the most current, technologically advanced products also heavily influences market leadership. Sometimes these drives are at odds. For instance, the organisation may be pressured to release a new product to remain in a market leadership position. However, if this product has not been adequately tested it may create customer dissatisfaction and complaints. The technical support function is in a critical position in maintaining long-term client loyalty, but also has limited control over release dates for new products. Despite this apparent lack of alignment, Arthur decided to proceed with his customer service strategy as he felt the market required them to be more customer-focused.

Internet Express SWOT analysis

Taken from a management retreat, the following represents a cross-section of the types of ideas that the team identified:

Strengths:

◆ commitment
◆ enthusiastic team
◆ strong visionary leadership
◆ organisation structure now integrated from multiple support structures to three support centres.

Weaknesses:

◆ lack of processes and procedures
◆ new company so no 'history' to refer to
◆ geographically dispersed (three centres worldwide)
◆ relatively young, inexperienced management team.

Opportunities:

◆ build a name for customer service
◆ lots of market growth with the expansion of the Internet
◆ ability to create own format and structure
◆ CEO who believes in the value of technical support.

Threats:

◆ lack of communication/coordination between engineering (who develop the product) and technical support
◆ if the product is unreliable it strains resources

- different physical location from headquarters – out of sight/out of mind
- other competitors entering the market and providing better service.

Arthur decided he would define his customer service strategy to capitalise on the strengths and opportunities, and that he would try to identify specific tactics to minimise weaknesses and reduce threats. He felt that customer service in today's technical world was non-negotiable, and that money and time invested in this area was as important as investment in new tools and technologies.

Internet Express strategy and slogan

The strategy that was decided for the technical support group was to move from a 'drive fast, take chances' mentality to a 'treat the customer as you would wish to be treated' culture. He felt that this strategy included both internal and external customers, and captured the important meaning behind a customer-focused approach. The purpose of Worldwide Support Services is to maximise customer retention. The slogan the team chose was: 'One team, one centre, the best solution'.

This slogan was meant to unite the three teams, and the various levels of support (front line level one, back line level two and product support level three). It also focused on the solutions aspect of meeting customer needs: exceeding customer expectations is not just about fixing the problem. It includes providing the best resolution for the customer. That resolution could be as simple as listening to the customer venting, creating an action plan or providing necessary information.

Internet Express values

The group decided to adhere to the company values that were clearly defined and located on posters, business cards, etc. The team thought that changing these values might cause confusion for the engineers and appear to not be aligned with the overall corporate direction. Samples of these corporate values were:

- Do the right things – don't just do things right.
- The only constant is change.
- Treat others as you wish to be treated.

Customer service as a key result area

Internet Express defined its key result areas as follows:

1. Customer service.

2. Problem resolution.
3. Process re-engineering.
4. People management.
5. Research and development.
6. People.
7. Financial requirements.
8. Internal communication.
9. Marketing service contracts.

A technical support department should always have a customer service key results area.

Communicating the Internet Express strategy

Arthur used various techniques to communicate the customer service strategy:

◆ He held all-hands meetings at the three support centres.
◆ He distributed via e-mail his overall goals for the coming year, which showed a strong emphasis on customer satisfaction.
◆ He instituted a 'high achievers' award for those who had demonstrated exceptional service skills (see Chapter 10).
◆ He held regular meetings with those who reported directly to him where they discussed customer success stories.
◆ He published regularly any positive customer feedback.
◆ He created screen-savers with the slogan and strategy.
◆ He introduced a skills-enhancement training programme for everyone who had contact with customers (see Chapter 5). _____

Discussion points

1. To what extent is your corporate vision and mission statement in alignment with instituting a customer service strategy? What facets of these statements would support and which hinder a customer service initiative?
2. When you conducted the SWOT analysis, what organisational factors were strengths in providing exceptional customer service and which were limitations? What factors existed outside of the organisation that would necessitate and support a customer service imperative, and which would possibly inhibit its implementation?
3. Based on the answers to questions 1 and 2, is a customer

service strategy realistic and feasible at this time? What is the main business driver? Is senior management committed to customer service or are they paying lip service to the idea? How could the service direction be made a reality?

4. If the answers to question 3 are positive, what steps will you take to decide the most important customer service values?

5. Have you evaluated the responsibilities of your team/function and included customer service as a key result area? Does this key result area appear to be in conflict with any other categories?

6. How will you start the internal communications campaign: How will you use face-to-face, e-mail and written communication? How will you ensure that communication is ongoing and consistent in terms of message and delivery?

Summary

In this chapter you have learned about the most important steps to define a customer service strategy:

◆ Any customer service strategy has to be in alignment with the company's vision and mission. If it isn't, the strategy will not succeed.

◆ It is important to conduct a SWOT analysis for the company when implementing a customer service strategy. If not, you may be unrealistic about your ability to deliver on the promise of exceptional service.

◆ Once you have made the commitment to exceeding customer expectations, you need to create a clear customer service strategy with a slogan or 'mantra' that captures the spirit of the service experience.

◆ In order to facilitate excellent internal service, you need to define your internal customer service values, which provides the foundation for excellent external service.

◆ To ensure that customer service remains a priority and visible at all times, one of the key result areas (the categories into which the workload for a team, function or organisation fit) needs to be customer service.

◆ When you have completed this preliminary work, you need to communicate, communicate and communicate with every tool and methodology at your disposal, on a consistent, ongoing basis.

CHAPTER 4

Hiring the Right People

I n order to consistently deliver outstanding customer service, we need not only a clear strategy but to find the right people, with the critical skills required to provide exceptional service. In this chapter we will discuss how to manage the recruitment process to identify and meet the specific requirements for the job. The recruitment process involves more than just placing an advertisement! Then we'll look at specific interviewing strategies to ensure we select the right people, those with a customer focus. Finally we will reveal how our companies in the case studies were able to hire the right people for their teams. With the best will in the world, if you hire the wrong people any customer change programme will not succeed: it's really hard to teach an elephant to dance!

Hiring or training customer service skills

When recruiting employees to provide customer service, the process often tends to concentrate more on skills, functional expertise, technical competence and knowledge rather than interpersonal skills. However, lack of a positive customer service attitude can drastically impact on customer service levels.

Going for interpersonal skills

The CEO of a high-tech company was in a cab in London with his Vice President of Sales. They were debating the critical competencies for sales people. He believed it was better to recruit people with the correct interpersonal skills/customer focus, and then provide them with technical training. His VP of Sales believed strongly that sales people should first have technical knowledge, and later develop the interpersonal and selling skills. The cab driver interrupted their debate and asked if he could act as the guinea pig. He had interpersonal and relationship building skills, but absolutely no technical knowledge. He joined the company and within five years became the number one sales person.

The message is this: when considering hiring people in roles where they need functional knowledge and interpersonal skills, it is better to hire the interpersonal skills and train the technical side rather than vice versa.

Managing the recruitment process

The recruitment process is made up of several important steps:

R: Requirements for the team
E: Employee/individual job requirements
C: Candidate sourcing
R: Reviewing background information
U: Understand the roles of the hiring team
I: Interview questions
T: Telephone screening.

Let's take a more detailed look at each of the steps within the recruitment process.

R: *Defining Requirements for the team*

Defining *individual responsibilities* requires building an overview of everything the team does, and from there determining the particular knowledge, skills, talents and abilities that need to be represented. As team requirements are always broader than the actual work itself, achieving the proper skill balance is not an easy task. The team needs a *balance of skills and competencies* in order to manage the workload effectively. Following is a sample list of skills needed on a team.

Technical knowledge/skills
- **Technical/professional knowledge:** level of technical and professional knowledge and/or education required to achieve team goals, particularly any specialised information.
- **Technical/professional skills:** level of technical and professional skills and experience in a particular function, such as marketing, sales, programming languages, statistical process control, etc.
- **Machine/software operation:** level of proficiency with necessary machines and/or software applications.

Communication skills

- **Oral communication:** the ability to effectively communicate verbally in individual or group situations.
- **Written communication:** the ability to express ideas clearly in writing.
- **Listening:** the ability to understand and use information from oral communication.

Interpersonal influence

- **Personal leadership:** using appropriate interpersonal styles and methods to guide individuals or groups towards task accomplishment.
- **Team orientation:** working with people to build high morale and group commitment to goals and objectives.
- **Persuasiveness/sales ability:** using appropriate interpersonal styles to gain agreement or acceptance of an idea, plan, activity or project. Ability to put people at ease and be liked and trusted; ability to get along with people.

Personality characteristics

- **Persistence:** adhering to a course of action, belief or purpose until desired objective is achieved or is no longer realistically attainable.
- **Independence:** taking action on own convictions rather than deferring to opinions of others.
- **Responsiveness:** reacting quickly to suggestions, influences, appeals and efforts.

Management

- **Planning and organising:** establishing a course of action for self and/or others to accomplish a specific goal; planning proper assignments of personnel and/or appropriate allocation of resources.
- **Control:** establishing procedures to monitor and/or regulate processes, tasks or activities of employees; taking action to monitor the results of delegated assignments or projects.

Problem-solving/decision-making

- **Analysis:** relating and comparing data from different sources, identifying issues, securing relevant information and identifying relationships.

- ◆ **Creativity:** generating many ideas; developing solutions to problems.
- ◆ **Resourcefulness:** acting effectively and imaginatively in difficult situations.
- ◆ **Judgement:** developing alternative courses of action and making decisions based on logical assumptions which reflect factual information.

Motivational
- ◆ **Job motivation:** gaining personal satisfaction from activities and responsibilities of a job.
- ◆ **Initiative:** self-starting, actively attempting to influence events and achieve goals.
- ◆ **Energy:** maintaining a high activity level.

Exercise	Build your team's capabilities list. Consider the team that is providing service to your customers. Using the skills presented above list the critical abilities, knowledge and characteristics required for your team to achieve the desired results.
	1. Major responsibilities (from key result areas see Chapter 3 on strategy).
	2. Team responsibilities (desired/required):
	  i technical knowledge/skills
	  ii communication skills
	  iii interpersonal influence
	  iv personality characteristics
	  v management
	  vi problem-solving/decision-making
	  vii motivational.

E:	*Employee/individual job requirements*

When hiring service providers, it's your responsibility to ensure that the person you hire is capable of doing the job as defined by the job description. Therefore, once a job description has been developed, specific *job requirements* should be identified for each position.

Job requirements are the required and desired qualities that are necessary for success on the job. Job requirements include:

◆ education
◆ work/related experience
◆ skills and knowledge
◆ job characteristics (the most important job requirements are the job characteristics).

One tool that will help you evaluate applicants is a job requirements checklist. (Figure 5 shows a thorough list of *characteristics/job dimensions* that you can use to create your own checklist.

Exercise   Building individual job requirements:
1. Think about a particular service provider role.
2. For that role, define the major responsibilities.
3. Then define the job dimensions that are important for this job role.
4. Pay particular attention to selecting the critical job characteristics for that role. Try to limit these to four.

Job requirements checklist

Position:
1. Major responsibilities (from job description).
2. Job dimensions (desired/required):
   i   education
   ii   work experience
   iii   skills and knowledge
   iv   job characteristics.

C: *Candidate sourcing*

The purpose of a sourcing strategy is to increase the *quality and quantity* of the pool of candidates available to you to screen and interview. Depending on the size of your company, it is possible to source candidates both internally and externally.

Internal sourcing involves placing a job-posting internally to identify potential candidates who are in other departments in the company. There are many benefits of internal sourcing including:
◆ The candidate has prior knowledge of the company and its products and services.

Communications	Oral communication	Effective expression in individual or group situations
	Written communication	Clear, effective expression of ideas in writing
	Listening	Understanding and use of information from oral communication
Personal/ motivational	Job motivation	The extent to which activities and responsibilities in a job result in personal satisfaction
	Work standards	Sets high goals or standards of performance
	Self-organisation	Effectively schedules own time and activities
	Initiative	Self-starting, actively attempts to influence events and reach goals
	Tolerance for ambiguity	Functions successfully in situations where information is vague, conflicting, altogether lacking or overwhelming
	Energy	Maintains a high activity level
	Attention to detail	Identifies and maintains required action of individual elements of a situation, no matter how small
	Alertness	Attends to all aspects of the environment while working; anticipates problems
	Integrity	Maintains social, ethical and organisational norms in job-related activities
	Patience	Maintains mature problem-solving attitude and objectivity while dealing with conflict, uncomfortable conditions, hostility or time demands
	Self-confidence	Trusts in him/herself and ability
Interpersonal	Assertiveness	Maturely expresses opinions in spite of others' status or position; effectively deals with conflict
	Sensitivity	Displays actions that indicate a consideration for the feelings and needs of others
	Leadership	Uses appropriate interpersonal styles and methods to guide individuals or groups towards task accomplishment

	Persistence	Adheres to a course of action, belief or purpose until desired objective is achieved or is no longer realistically attainable
	Persuasiveness/ sales ability	Uses appropriate interpersonal styles to gain agreement or acceptance of an idea, plan or project
	Flexibility/ versatility	Maintains effectiveness in varying environments and with varying tasks, responsibilities or people; able to do many different things competently
	Rapport building	Able to put people at ease and be liked and trusted; able to get along with people
	Team orientation	Works with people to build high morale and group commitment to goals and objectives
	Independence	Takes action on own convictions rather than deferring to opinions of others
	Responsiveness	Reacts quickly to suggestions, influences, appeals and efforts
	Resilience	Handles disappointment and/or rejection while maintaining effectiveness
Management	Planning and organising	Establishes a course of action for self and/or others to accomplish a specific goal; plans proper assignments of personnel and/or appropriate allocation of resources
	Delegation	Uses others effectively; allocates decision-making and other responsibilities to the appropriate people
	Control	Establishes procedures to monitor and/or regulate processes, tasks or activities of employees; takes action to monitor results of delegated assignments or projects
Problem-solving decision-making	Analysis	Relates and compares data from different sources, identifying issues, securing relevant information and identifying relationships

Creativity	Generates many ideas; develops unique solutions to problems
Logic	Clear reasoning and consistent thinking
Resourcefulness	Acts effectively and imaginatively in difficult situations
Judgement	Develops alternative courses of action and makes decisions based on logical assumptions which reflect factual information
Decisiveness	Readiness to make decisions, render judgements, take action or commit him/herself as necessary
Risk-taking	Willing to take course of action not taken before, or involving a deliberate gamble to achieve a recognised benefit or advantage
Organisational sensitivity	Perceives the impact and the implications of decisions on other components of the organisation

Fig. 5. List of characteristics/job dimensions.

- Hopefully, the candidate has a documented performance path within the organisation.
- There are internal reference sources to consult regarding the candidate's abilities and approach.

There may also be some disadvantages to using internal sourcing:
- The other internal manager may not want to release the candidate.
- You may have to be more flexible in terms of a start date.
- Occasionally, internal candidates are 'problem children' who are being moved around rather than fired.

Most organisations have an internal recruitment policy and human resources can normally provide details of this process.

External sourcing: there is a wide variety of sourcing channels open to you when trying to hire externally. These include:
- *Unsolicited CVs* sent by applicants who have targeted your company.

- **Advertising.** An extremely cost-effective way to source candidates if managed correctly. It can include newspapers, both local and regional, Internet, association newsletters (in your field), radio, magazines, university job listings, etc. Whichever medium you select the advertisement must be written to clearly describe the job requirements you identified earlier. Often companies have arrangements with specific agencies that help to put together and place recruitment advertising.
- **Recruitment agencies/search firms.** There are two types of recruitment agencies – retainer and contingency:
  - retainer firms are retained by the company to locate qualified candidates for specific positions. They are paid a standard fee by the company regardless of whether the candidates are hired.
  - contingency firms are paid a fee only when a candidate presented by the contingency firm is hired.
- **Recruiters.** Contract recruiters can be used on an hourly basis.
- **Networking/employee referrals.** One of the best sources of candidates is through word-of-mouth. This process can be maximised by:
  - networking with other managers to share information about openings.
  - talking to and e-mailing current employees in case they know a good candidate.
  - talking to previous employees.
  - checking with your HR manager.
  - providing cash rewards for internal referrals.
  - keeping your eyes open for great service providers when you are a customer with other organisations. Remember you can train technical skills if you find someone with interpersonal skills.
- **Colleges/universities and training schemes.** Many organisations run extensive campus recruitment campaigns, often managed by the director of recruitment.
- **Associations/professional organisations/user groups/conferences.** Increasingly, professional organisations can be an excellent source of candidates, particularly if there is specific technical knowledge required – just watch for the interpersonal skills too.

Make sure you use as many sources as you can when recruiting for your team.

Exercise

Sourcing candidates:

What sourcing channels could you use for a particular position you can think of?

- unsolicited CVs
- advertising
- recruitment agencies/search firms
- recruiters
- networking/employee referrals
- colleges/universities and training schemes
- associations/professional organisations/user groups/conferences.

R: *Reviewing background information*

Prior to the interview, the basic written tool available to you will be the *CV* and/or the *application form*. The CV is the key document for outside applicants.

The first step in reviewing this written documentation is to identify any information that is incomplete or confusing to you. To clarify your understanding, you will want to ask the applicant about these items prior to the beginning of your face-to-face interview to clarify your understanding. *Red flags* on the written materials are:

- preference for a job that is not presently available
- incomplete information, such as missing phone numbers, street addresses, postal codes
- stated salary requirements clearly not within the guidelines of the open position
- gaps in work or education history
- lack of career progress.

U: *Understanding the roles of the hiring team*

A key part in preparing for the interview is to select the hiring team, then:

- decide roles and responsibilities in the hiring process

  - discuss, as a group, the job requirements for the position, particularly the characteristics, and develop legal interview questions
  - allocate the job requirements for interviews to team members to reduce repetition
  - decide the evaluation process.

I: *Interview questions*

The way we gather data about a candidate's capabilities is to ask questions about the job requirements. To ensure the diversity of questions, and to help gather the information required, it's normally a good idea to prepare interview questions in advance. Figure 6 shows some examples of *questions for each job requirement category.*

T: *Telephone screening*

The telephone is an extremely *cost-effective* and *time-efficient* tool in the recruitment and selection process. Often you will conduct preliminary telephone screenings to:
  - narrow down the pool of candidates
  - clarify missing or incomplete information
  - determine further interest from a candidate
  - assess compensation requirements and availability.

Guidelines:
  - Be sure to have the job requirements checklist handy.
  - Prepare a list of questions.
  - Move through the questions, listening.
  - Have a telephone screening form to jot down any notes.
  - Select questions based on top-priority job requirements.
  - Check availability, compensation requirements, interest and relocation status (if appropriate).

The interview process

The next step in hiring the right candidates is understanding how to conduct an interview.

The interview process includes the following steps:

Communications	Oral communication	• What different approaches do you use when talking with different people? How do you know you are getting your point across? • What are some of the most complex processes/rules/products/situations you have had to explain to other people?
	Written communication	• What are some of the most important reports you've written? What reactions did they get? Were they hard to write? Why? • What are some of the most difficult writing assignments you have been given or have taken upon yourself? Explain.
	Listening	• Give some examples from your past jobs when you had to rely on information given to you orally to get the job done. • How do you show others (managers/customers/peers) you are listening to them?
Personal motivational	Job motivation	• Give examples of experiences in your present job that have been satisfying, dissatisfying. • Give an example of when you worked the hardest and felt the greatest achievement.
	Work standards	• What are your standards of success in your job? What have you done to meet them? • Compare and contrast the times when you did work which was above standard and times it was below standard.
	Self-organisation	• What do you do when your time schedule is upset by unforeseen circumstances? Give examples. • What are your objectives for this year? Who else knows about them? What are you doing to reach them? How are you progressing?
	Initiative	• Describe ways you've changed your current job. • What changes have you tried to implement in your area of

		responsibility? What have you done to get them started?
	Tolerance for ambiguity	• Describe a time when you had to make a decision without all the necessary information. • Describe a time when you had to perform under conflicting directions. How did you deal with the conflict?
	Energy	• How do you catch up on a backlog of work after a holiday? • Describe the last time you felt thoroughly exhausted.
	Attention to detail	• Describe your system for controlling errors in your work. • We've all had times when we just couldn't get everything done on time. When and why has this happened to you?
	Alertness	• How do you stay familiar with the technical aspects of the products at your job? • Describe a time when you predicted changes in the work environment before they happened.
	Integrity	• Salespeople frequently have to oversell a product to make an important sale. Can you give examples of when you did this? • How far do you think the average salesperson in your field goes to make a sale? How far have you gone?
	Patience	• Describe a time when you chose not to speak out about something. Describe a time when you did. What was the difference between the two situations? • Give an example of when you had to wait for an important decision or piece of information. How did that affect you?
	Self-confidence	• Give an example of when your self-confidence led you to take action others might not have. • Give an example of when your lack of self-confidence prevented you from taking action.

Interpersonal influence	Assertiveness	• Describe a time when you had to tell your manager some bad news. What happened? • Describe a recent time when you had to deal with an angry or impatient person. What did you do? How did they react?
	Sensitivity	• Describe some situations when you wish you had acted differently with someone at work. What did you do? What happened? • What unpopular decisions have you made recently? How did others respond? How did that make you feel?
	Leadership	• Tell me about some of the toughest groups from whom you have had to get cooperation. Did you have any formal authority? What did you do? • Tell me about a new policy or idea you recently implemented which was considerably different from standard procedure. What approach did you take to get your employees to go along with it?
	Persistence	• What are some big obstacles you have had to overcome to get where you are today? How did you overcome them? • Describe a time when you were too persistent. What happened? How could you have improved the outcome?
	Persuasiveness/ sales ability	• What are some of the best ideas you ever sold to a superior/peer/subordinate? What was your approach? • What are some of the best ideas you tried but failed to sell to a superior/peer/subordinate? What was your approach? Why did they fail?
	Flexibility/ versatility	• When have you edited your normal behaviour to meet the needs and desires of others? • Describe a situation when you were required to work with someone you disliked.

	Rapport building	• How did you go about developing rapport with customers, co-workers and people from other parts of the organisation at your present job? Examples. • We've all had to work with difficult people. Tell me when this has happened to you. Why was that person difficult? How did you handle the situation?
	Team orientation	• Describe a situation when you developed a group into a strong working team. • Tell me about a time when you had difficulty getting others to establish a common approach to a problem. What did you do? What was the outcome?
	Independence	• Tell me about some rules, policies or approaches at work you didn't agree with and what you did about them. • What do you do in your job that isn't covered in the job description?
	Responsiveness	• Describe a situation when you were too late in your response. What did you do? • Give an example of a time when you had to respond to a suggestion, request, etc. How quickly were you able to react and in what way?
	Resilience	• What have been the biggest disappointments at your job? How have you coped with them?
	Sales	• What percentage of your calls result in a sale? How do you feel when someone turns you down?
Management	Planning and organising	• What kinds of project planning and administration do you do in your current job? • What is your procedure for keeping track of items needing your attention?
	Delegation	• How often do you assign work to other people? What do you assign? To whom? • Who is 'minding the store'

		while you are here? How were they selected? Why? How will you know how they performed?
	Control	• What procedures do you use for evaluating your employees' performances? • Describe the basic content of your staff meetings. How are action items assigned? How often are these meetings held?
Problem-solving/decision-making	Analysis	• What problem are you currently working on that came as a surprise? How much advance notice did you have of the problem? Why was it such a surprise? What steps did you take after you identified it? • Describe the biggest problems you've faced in the last six months. How did you handle them?
	Creativity	• What has been the most creative accomplishment in your current job? • When have you used creativity to solve a problem at work? How did it turn out?
	Logic	• Tell me about a complex decision you recently had to make. What were the key elements to consider? How did you make your decision? What was the outcome? • Describe a situation where you had to organise a large number of details. How did you prioritise your work? What could you have done to make things go smoother?
	Resourcefulness	• Describe a situation when you were blocked from reaching a goal or non-negotiable deadline. What did you do? • When you first started your current job, how did you build your network of resources? How long did it take?
	Judgement	• Tell me about a decision when you had to balance multiple priorities. How did you weigh each of the factors?

		• What were the hardest decisions you've had to make at your present job? Tell me about them. What alternatives did you consider?
	Decisiveness	• What are the most difficult decisions you've made in the last six months? Why were they difficult? • How have you made important decisions affecting your career?
	Risk-taking	• Tell me about the riskiest management decision you've made (present/previous company). How long did it take to gather the information to make the decision? How long after that to make the decision? What were the results? • Describe the biggest calculated risk you have taken in your job.
	Organisational sensitivity	• Let's go over the organisational chart you drew for me. Tell me whom, if anyone, you frequently come into contact with in each of these departments and for what reason. • How often do you make decisions that affect departments other than your own? What kinds of decisions are these?

Fig. 6.   Questions for each job requirement category.

Opening the interview
◆ create a relaxed atmosphere
◆ explain the interview process
◆ clarify missing or confusing information from the CV
◆ Give brief information about the company and the position.

Collecting information from the candidate
◆ open-ended questions
◆ probing for specifics
◆ active listening
◆ paraphrasing
◆ closed questions
◆ rapport

- silence
- note-taking.

Providing information
- answer questions about the job, the company and the work environment.

Closing the interview
- explain the next steps
- thank the applicant.

Evaluating the candidate
- avoid evaluation pitfalls
- discard inappropriate information
- conduct the evaluation asap.

1 Opening the interview

There are four steps you should follow to open the interview.

a Create a relaxed atmosphere:
- arrange for no interruptions: forward your phone, shut your door
- don't keep the candidate waiting
- conduct the interview in private
- conduct the interview in private/business surroundings
- if possible, greet the applicant in the reception area
- make some small-talk
- perhaps offer the applicant a drink.

b Explain the interview process:
- introduce yourself and your title
- briefly explain the title and position you hold
- explain that you will be, initially, asking most of the questions
- explain the sequencing of the interviews and explain who will be doing what.

c Clarify missing or confusing information from CV.

d Give brief information about the company and the position:
- size
- job responsibilities
- department.

2   *Collecting information from the candidate*

This is the most important part of the interview. Too often, inexperienced interviewers talk about the company and the position instead of collecting as much data as possible from the candidate.

There are eight basic techniques used to collect and confirm information. Many of these techniques are also used to manage the customer interaction and will be described in more detail in Chapter 6.

a. *Open-ended questions*, asked to learn more about the applicant. Open-ended questions cannot be answered by a yes or no. They begin with such words/phrases as: who, what, where, when, why, how, tell me about . . . , describe . . . , in what way . . . , etc.

 Open-ended questions are effective at getting applicants to share their thoughts, feelings and opinions. They stimulate two-way conversation and stop the interview from sounding as if it were an interrogation.

b *Probing for specifics.* You have used the opening questions to identify specific job requirements. Now you need to follow up the applicant's answers with appropriate questions and interviewing techniques. For instance, if a candidate said 'In my last job there were always irate customers calling' you could probe for specifics with such questions as 'Tell me about a specific irate customer situation. What did you do in that situation? What could have been done to reduce the number of irate customer calls? What did you try to do to reduce the root cause of some of these problems?'

c *Active listening*, which in an interview is a key communications tool for building positive relationships and assessing a candidate's fit within a position. The aim of active listening is to focus entirely on the candidate and be aware of content and the underlying meaning being expressed. It is important to separate your listening from the evaluation process. It is often tempting to begin to 'rate' the candidate instead of listening with an objective framework to what is being said. Beginning the evaluation process may result in a distorted perception. I don't like the person: now I see more things that cause me to dislike him/her even more!

d   *Paraphrasing* is restating in your own words what the other person has said. The simplest way to paraphrase is to listen without interrupting, and then follow up with a sentence such as 'So, what you're saying is . . . ' Paraphrasing enables you to determine whether or not you have accurately understood the applicant.

e   *Closed questions* are used in the interview to verify data, limit an applicant's answer and move from one discussion to another.

f   *Rapport:*
   ◆   encourages an applicant to open up
   ◆   uses words and phrases such as: 'Oh?, I understand, uh huh, of course, interesting.'
   ◆   We also build rapport by mirroring body language, pace and tone.

g   *Silence* in the interview allows the applicant to gather and formulate thoughts, while at the same time giving them an opportunity to respond. Silence can last from four to twelve seconds depending on the complexity of the question and the profile of the candidate. See Chapter 6 for more information.

h   *Note-taking* in the interview will help you remember, retain focus and provide a useful written record when evaluating the candidate. Following are some guidelines for note-taking:
   ◆   ask for permission
   ◆   don't write notes continuously
   ◆   use key words
   ◆   highlight areas you want to return to
   ◆   do not write on CV or application.

3   *Providing information and answering questions*

When you are satisfied you have gathered all the information you need from the applicant, be prepared to answer questions relating to:
   ◆   the job
   ◆   the company
   ◆   the working environment.

4   Closing the interview

You have now learned the basic techniques for planning, opening and conducting an interview. Once you have obtained all the information you need about each of the performance criteria, it is time to end the interview.

There are two basic steps to closing an interview:

First explain the steps that follow:

+ Review the hiring process.
+ Tell the applicant what will happen next.
+ Tell the applicant how and when he/she will be notified of the hiring decision.

Secondly thank the applicant:

+ Thank the applicant for his/her cooperation and interest in the company.
+ Show them to the reception area.

It is best to not volunteer too much more information regarding the evaluation of the applicant. You want to try to remain as neutral as possible and not give the applicant any false encouragement or negative feedback. Remember that no matter what your final hiring decision may be, the applicant could be a current or potential customer. Be nice.

Finally, there may be times when you feel it is appropriate to sell the benefits of working for your organisation. While this may be appropriate in some instances, it is still wise to remain as neutral as possible regarding your final hiring decision.

Exercise

Conducting the interview:

1. Review the job requirements checklist you prepared earlier.
2. Pick one specific job aspect/characteristic that is critical for your team members to have in order to provide exceptional customer service.
3. Conduct a mini-interview to gather information from a partner to assess his/her competence in this area.
4. Remember to:
   + ask open-ended questions
   + probe for specifics
   + listen actively

- ◆ paraphrase
- ◆ use closed questions
- ◆ use rapport
- ◆ use silence
- ◆ write notes.

5. Debrief with your partner to discuss what you could have done more effectively.

---

5 *Evaluating the applicant*

Once the interview is complete, it's time to evaluate the applicant and the information you have gathered. If at all possible, it's best to evaluate immediately following the interview. Try to avoid evaluation while the interview is in progress. To do so may result in a failure to cover all the job requirements. In addition, forming opinions and making judgements during the interview itself may lead you to ask only questions that confirm your feeling or hypothesis . . . a sort of self-fulfilling prophecy.

It's a good idea to jot down a few notes during the interview that will jog your memory during the evaluation process. While conducting the evaluation, refer to the job requirements checklist to further validate the information you received during the interview.

There are several major *pitfalls to be avoided* when evaluating the information you receive from an applicant.

- ◆ Bias. Try to be aware of any attitudes, prejudices or personal feelings held towards certain groups of people.
- ◆ First impressions. Beware of latching on to a single remark made by an applicant or a single attitude that you might consider inappropriate. In other words, contrary to conventional wisdom, don't go on initial gut feelings. More often than not this will lead to a tendency to 'over-test' your hypothesis and ask leading questions that will not provide accurate evidence. You may find yourself attributing to the applicant ideas, attitudes and feelings that are really your own.
- ◆ Mirror image. Just as bias and snap judgements can cause you to evaluate an applicant negatively, the mirror image pitfall can have exactly the opposite effect. By mirror image we mean the transference of your own self-image onto another person. We

all have a tendency to gravitate towards people with tastes and opinions similar to our own. In the interviewing process this tendency might result in evaluating an applicant more favourably than the facts warrant.

Inappropriate information: when evaluating an applicant you will use two sources of information.
1. Information actually reported by the applicant.
2. Observations you made of the applicant's behaviour during the interview.

Remember the information is valid only if it relates to specific job requirements. Do not use information that is irrelevant to successful job performance or that is drawn from a conclusion that cannot be backed up with facts.

Here are some examples of appropriate and inappropriate back-up information:

◆ Appropriate: *The applicant found it difficult to make decisive answers. They didn't know what they liked or disliked about previous jobs, didn't know whether or not to go back to university, stay in retailing or move into direct sales.*
◆ Inappropriate: *Applicant seemed wishy-washy.*
◆ Appropriate: *Applicant explained in detail a system for monitoring sales volume.*
◆ Inappropriate: *Applicant showed 'know-how'.*

Exercise

Appropriate or inappropriate exercise.
Decide which of the statements below are appropriate information on which to base an evaluation.
–   applicant seems mature
–   applicant describes system he/she set up for current job
–   applicant lacks self-confidence
–   applicant likes working alone on research for large projects
–   applicant is people-oriented
–   applicant verbalises clear-cut sales strategies when explaining interest in sales.

(Answers below.)
When you have selected the candidate you think is the best fit, you're ready to include that person in your customer service culture through training, a clear orientation to the company and

by providing rewards and recognition to enhance individual performance. We will be looking at these subjects in a later chapter, but let's look at how the companies in our case studies ensured they hired the right people.

Answers: The appropriate answers are marked with an **a**, the inappropriate answers with an **i**.

- applicant seems mature: no data to back up statement: **i**
- applicant describes system he/she set up for current job: **a**
- applicant lacks self confidence: no data to back up statement: **i**
- applicant likes working alone on research for large projects: **a**
- applicant is people oriented: no data and what does that mean anyway?! **i**
- applicant verbalises clear-cut sales strategies when explaining interest in sales: **a**

Case Study: Cleanworks: hiring the right people

Cleanworks was in the enviable position of being able to hire its entire team from scratch – an unusual situation. As the company had defined customer service as one of its keys to business success, the definition of customer service competencies for all roles was explicitly stated.

Managing the recruitment process: Some of the competencies they identified for their van drivers were as shown in Figure 7.

The other job characteristics were identified as:

◆ initiative
◆ technical skills
◆ organisation skills
◆ team player
◆ accountability.

The company decided to source candidates not only from the dry cleaning and laundry industry, but also from other low-income/relatively unskilled labour industries such as fast food, office cleaning, house cleaning, etc. They primarily relied on advertising, and posted ads at college campuses, then hired an hourly recruiter to help screen the CVs.

On the hiring team they used not only the internal management team but customer service consultants to help filter the candidates for customer service focus. They created a list of questions, as shown in Figure 8, and allocated different questions to different team members: the internal managers focused on questions relating to technical and organisational skills, the external customer service consultants focused on questions relating to communication and

Communication	Communicates effectively	◆ Demonstrates effective inter-personal communication skills ◆ Communicates in an open, straightforward manner
	Focuses on the situation	◆ Remains objective ◆ Focuses on the situation, issues, or behaviour, not the person
	Listens effectively	◆ Demonstrates active-listening skills by asking for clarification ◆ Communicates using verbal and non-verbal cues
Customer orientation	Exceeds customer expectations	◆ Consistently works to ensure the highest level of customer satisfaction
	Effectively manages customer expectations	◆ Works with customers to better understand their needs and expectations ◆ Negotiates and communicates appropriate timelines for deliverables ◆ Continually seeks customer feedback (internally and externally)
	Customer focus	◆ Establishes effective working relationships with customers, both internally and externally ◆ Identifies and takes appropriate action on customer needs ◆ Seeks ways to increase customer satisfaction

Fig. 7.   Sample competencies identification checklist.

customer service.

Managing the interview process: The team discovered that by allocating questions to different team members they were able to hold more productive interviews and to more effectively contrast the answers from various candidates.

They created an interview evaluation form (shown in Figure 9) where they rated each candidate against the criteria with a brief explanation as to their rationale for the rating. They met immediately after each interview so that the ideas were fresh in their minds and charted the composite score for each candidate. They discussed any discrepancies and always placed a greater emphasis on the customer service and communication skills in the final hiring decision. They made a point of questioning whether their rationale for rating each candidate was objective. The group discussion helped to eliminate some of the inherent bias in the evaluation process.

Communication	Communicates effectively	◆ Describe how you would communicate bad news to a customer ◆ How would you empathise in this situation?
	Focuses on the situation	◆ Describe a situation when a customer has become angry and begun attacking you personally. What did you do? ◆ How did you prevent the hostility from escalating?
Customer orientation	Exceeds customer expectations	◆ Describe a situation when you have exceeded customer expectations ◆ How did the customer respond?
	Effectively manages expectations	◆ Explain a scenario when you had to communicate to a customer that the date they were expecting a task to be completed had slipped ◆ What did you say to set more realistic expectations?
Initiative	Takes initiative to make things better	◆ Describe a situation when something was not working and you made changes to make it work ◆ Why had no one else made these changes?
	Demonstrates creativity	◆ What would you say has been the most creative accomplishment in your last position? ◆ What kinds of problems have people recently called on you to solve? Tell me about your contributions to solving them
Team player	Maintains constructive relationships with others	◆ Describe a situation when you had a conflict with a co-worker ◆ What was the source of the conflict? How did you resolve it?
	Recognises others	◆ Give me an example of a piece of positive feedback you gave to another team member ◆ How did he/she respond to the feedback?

Fig. 8. Sample questions for hiring customer service focused staff.

Case study: Kitchen Barn: hiring the right people

Kitchen Barn had always used a clear job description when hiring Sales Associates, and had customised the job requirements form for their audience.

Because of the change in business focus, they realised they needed to create a new position, a Product Expert, to act as an adviser in each store on the furniture and furnishings questions. Part of the job requirements checklist is listed in Figure 10.

Criteria	Rating: 1 = excellent 10 = poor	Reasons/Notes
Communication		
Customer orientation		
Initiative		
Technical skills		
Organisation skills		
Team player		
Accountability		

Fig. 9.   Interview evaluation form.

JOB REQUIREMENTS CHECKLIST

Position: Product Expert
Major responsibilities (from job description)
• Act as adviser to store personnel on measuring and installing curtains and purchasing furniture.
• Organise literature to support questions.
• Other responsibilities the same as Sale Associates, i.e. operating the register, working on the shop floor, inventory management, etc.

Job dimensions (desired/required)
Education:
• Bachelors Degree desired.

Work experience:
• Time spent as an interior designer required.
• Work in some sort of furniture/furnishings industry, preferably on the consumer side

Skills and knowledge:
• Knowledge of the furniture industry
• Interior design skills

Job characteristics:
• Initiative
• Listening
• Persuasiveness/sales ability.

Fig. 10.   Part of a job requirements checklist.

While the focus of this job was definitely more technical, the job requirements checklist ensured that technical competence was not substituted for interpersonal/service skills.

To reinforce the importance of selecting the correct people, Gary invested in training all the District Managers in behavioural interviewing at the Store

Managers Annual Conference. In this session, District Managers created additional questions that could be used in the interview process to identify the necessary data.

Case Study: Internet Express: hiring the right people

Arthur felt that individuals in this area of work tended to be more technical, could 'talk a good line' in the interview, but tended to demonstrate arrogance when interacting with the customer.

For this reason he decided to use an assessment centre, to complement the behavioural interviewing approach that was described in this chapter. Running an assessment centre involves creating scenarios that future employees might face in the world of work and then allowing them to role-play how they would respond in each situation. Assessment centres tend to avoid some verbal camouflage that abounds in interviews. Have you ever interviewed someone and been really impressed, but then when they start you wonder how you could have been so wrong?

Some of the scenarios presented at the assessment centre were:

◆ Instructing a really non-technical customer how to install a piece of software. (This can cause technical people to get impatient.)

◆ Posing a problem, that although not complex required several questions for an effective analysis (to assess to what extent the engineer was making assumptions).

◆ Describing a scenario with multiple agendas (to assess whether the engineer was only in 'fix-it' mode).

These scenarios had been developed for the personal service skills training, so there were considerable timesavings, plus an alignment between both approaches. Arthur used an interview team, where each person focused on one of the specific job requirements: one person was the technical expert, one probed for problem-solving abilities, one for the ability to successfully defuse irate customers, etc. This meant that there was an efficient interview process, and interviewers were better able to compare and contrast different candidates.

The result from this approach was that some really top-flight technical applicants were not hired, due to their approach with the customer, and some less seasoned but willing applicants were hired instead. _____

Discussion points

1. How do you currently decide the mix of talents and skills required on your team? What formal processes, if any, are there to ensure that you are hiring a balanced team to meet customer needs?

2. What job requirements have you identified as desired and required for your service providers? How different are these criteria from the selection categories or job descriptions you have used in the past? How could you formalise the use of these job requirements for your hiring process?

3. When it comes to recruiting people, what other sources of applicants could you investigate? What might be some new pools of talents that have the right skill mix, but are not necessarily in your industry? What untraditional approaches could you use to find new candidates?

4. How else could you use telephone screening in your hiring process? How could you screen out some of the unsuitable candidates before they are face-to-face with you?

5. What is your current interviewing process? How often do you speak more than 50 per cent of the time instead of asking the candidate questions? What could you do to raise the competence of those who interview?

6. How many questions have you created to use in the interview? What are the possibilities of creating scenarios and then using the assessment centre approach?

7. How effective are you at evaluating the candidate? To what extent do you wait until after the interview to make a decision, or do you decide within the first two minutes? What else could you do to avoid some of these evaluation pitfalls?

Summary

In this chapter we have highlighted the importance of hiring the right people in delivering exceptional service.

◆ We found it is better to hire the people with the correct interpersonal skills and then train the technical knowledge rather than vice versa.

◆ The recruitment process is made up of several important steps:
   R: Requirements for the team: define the overall mix of skills, knowledge and abilities.

E: Employee/individual job requirements: define specifically what each employee requires to be successful.

C: Candidate sourcing: use traditional and non-traditional channels to find the right people.

R: Reviewing background information: don't waste time face-to-face with candidates until you are sure you have all the necessary information from them.

U: Understand the roles of the hiring team: clearly define who does what and distribute questions accordingly.

I: Interview questions: create detailed, open-ended questions for each of the important job requirements.

T Telephone screening: use the telephone to narrow the field, it is cost- and time-effective.

- The interview process involves setting the scene, collecting as much information as possible from the candidate and providing any information they request. Finally, it is important to set realistic expectations with the applicant and to remember that today's applicant may be tomorrow's customer.
- When evaluating candidates it is important to wait until the end of the interview to avoid preconceptions. Avoid any biases and only use relevant, factual data.
- Time correctly invested in this area will make the rest of the service delivery process much easier.

CHAPTER 5

Developing Personal Service Skills

D elivering consistent outstanding personal service is a great challenge to service organisations because personal service is situational. It varies from one moment to the next and from one customer to the next. It also varies for the same customer at different times. As a result it's hard to predict, measure and enforce. This chapter will focus on the *communication process* and its *effect on personal service*, describing in some detail the attitude, words, delivery and body language we must use to communicate effectively with customers. In the next chapter we will demonstrate how we use other skills to manage the customer interaction, in order to set expectations correctly. Although many of the principles and techniques described in this chapter may seem to be nothing more than common sense, as we all know common sense is not necessarily common practice!

What is communication?

Communication is the exchange of information between sender and receiver. Norbert Weiner, in *The Human Use of Human Being – Cybernetics and Society*, writes 'Speech is a joint game between the talker and the listener against the forces of confusion.'

Too often communication is perceived as 'sending an e-mail' or talking to a customer, but for real communication to take place there needs to be feedback/response. In order for communication to be effective the message must be clear and the receiver must receive it, process it and act on it. Communication includes *the words said, the way they are said* and *the body language* used during the process. Communication skills will always require attention and refinement. E-mail is now a widely used method of communication and requires special attention when dealing with customers.

Exercise

One-way and two-way communication. The purpose of this exercise is to show the complexity of the communication process. Your task is to describe the diagram to your partner so that he/she can draw it. You will then repeat the exercise with a slight variation.

◆ The first time there will be only one-way communication: you can speak, but your partner can't ask questions, and you can't check for understanding.

◆ The second time you will use a different diagram, but there will be two-way communication. Your partner can ask questions and you can check for comprehension.

Instructions: first diagram

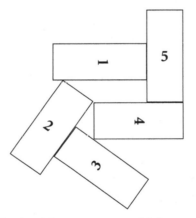

1. Sit back-to-back with your partner. Make sure he/she cannot see the diagram.
2. You have to describe the diagram, while your partner draws it.
3. The first time there is only one-way communication: you cannot ask questions and the person drawing cannot question your instructions.
4. You have five minutes to describe the diagram. If you finish before the five minutes are up, turn around and see how you did.
5. Compare pictures: how similar are they? What was missed? What was difficult about this exercise?

Instructions: second diagram

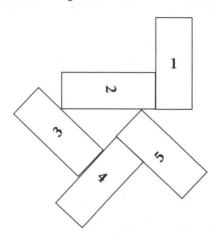

1. Now switch roles: you draw the diagram as your partner describes it. Again, make sure you cannot see it.
2. This time use two-way communication: you can ask questions and your partner can answer.
3. Take five minutes, then compare drawings again.
4. How did you do this time? What was easier? How accurate was the drawing?

The learning points from the exercise are as follows:
- Usually when we use this exercise in a training programme the one-way diagram is hopelessly inaccurate, and pairs normally give up after three minutes!
- With the two-way communication diagram the picture is normally more accurate; it takes more time, but often the drawing will be a 'mirror' of the diagram.

So the conclusions are:
- One-way communication is difficult. It takes less time, but produces less effective results. If the message is not understood, two way communication is needed to clarify it.
- When there is only one-way communication, the message can be clarified by providing a clear overview up front (there are five rectangles, all the same size, touching but not overlapping. The size of the rectangles is . . . They each have a number inside and the drawing is in landscape mode).

- In addition, word choice can enhance the effectiveness of the message being sent. For instance the use of north, south, east, west, the use of letters to describe the layout of the rectangles (the letter 'T'), being careful about technical language (angles, etc).
- Two-way communication normally produces better results, but is more time-consuming.
- Also, the second drawings are more accurate because of what was learned the first time.

The communication process

Normally when people are asked to identify the beginning of the communication process they say it begins with words or by getting the other person's attention. In reality, the communication process begins when the sender has an idea, thought or information that they wish to communicate. The sender must then formulate or organise the information, considering not only who will be the receiver, but what they wish to achieve as a result of sending the message. When the information has been mentally prepared, it is ready to be sent.

> When we are communicating with people face-to-face, we use both verbal and non-verbal communication.

Verbal communication refers to the actual *words we use* (word choice/dialogue), and the *way we say the words* (tone, pitch and volume). Non-verbal communication refers to *body language* (expressions, gestures and posture). When we communicate with someone with whom we have an ongoing relationship, *credibility* also plays a role. Credibility usually comes from the amount of connection, knowledge or reliability we recognise in the communicator. The statistics below show that on a first meeting body language is the main component of communication. When we have known someone for a while, credibility becomes more important.

	Initial meeting[1]	*Ongoing meetings[2]*
Words we use	7%	7%
Way we say the words	38%	14%
Body language	55%	24%
Credibility		55%

[1]Statistics: Mahrabian
[2]Statistics: Birdwhistle

When we send a message, if we're lucky the other person will receive it. However, too often filters such as bias, insufficient interest, rehearsing, lack of understanding and distraction prevent the listener from receiving the message. If the listener does receive the message, they then process it against their own reference bank and decode it appropriately in order to take action or provide a response.

Complexity of the process

The diagram above represents a simple explanation of the communication process. All the steps actually happen simultaneously. As the sender is thinking of an idea, they are formulating a sentence and possibly already sending the message. On the other end, the receiver is sending back a complex combination of responses during the whole transmission, while at the same time processing and decoding the information.

Lots of things can go wrong with the communication process. The sender may have an irrational idea, want to communicate incorrect data, or formulate the information erroneously for the receiver. By using the wrong words (too complex, too simple, jargon, slang), the sender could also offend, confuse, irritate or bore the receiver. In addition he/she might not deliver the words effectively (unclear enunciation, inappropriate body language). From the other side, the receiver might filter out the message or interpret it incorrectly because of their different frame of reference. The receiver could also provide a completely inappropriate response. The process is so complex that it is amazing anything is communicated accurately at all!

To complicate the process, cultural and individual diversity also contribute to communication confusion. Since many of us come from different countries and ethnic groups, our cultural values and language proficiencies can cause language barriers, misunderstandings and misinterpretations.

Let's look at some guidelines for improving the way we send the message when communicating with customers.

Communication attitude

'There is nothing good nor bad, that thinking doesn't make it so.'

Early Greek philosophers

Attitude is the basis for all the communication skills we will be discussing in this chapter. Your *attitude* and *approach* to your work can have a drastic influence on the effectiveness of communication. On the surface, attitude is the way you communicate your mood to others, but attitude starts in your head. It is the way you *mentally* approach situations.

Winner/loser tapes

The human brain is a little like a video recorder. When positive things happen, they are recorded in the brain as 'winner tapes'. For instance, I enjoy making presentations. Whenever I am thinking about a presentation I automatically visualise a positive outcome – I play a 'winner tape' and the result is usually how I envision it to be. In the same way, when negative things happen they are recorded in the brain as 'loser tapes'. For instance, I received a first-rate English education, which was theoretically sound but practically useless! As a result, when I am faced with fixing something that is broken, or even using the remote control for the TV, I automatically see myself failing – I play a 'loser tape' and more often than not fail. Remember there's a difference in choosing to play a loser tape and being a loser!

What makes us human is that at any one time we can choose which tape to play. When experiencing difficult situations in our personal lives, that decision can heavily influence not only the communication process, but also the outcome of the event. For instance, I have a friend who in one year had a miscarriage, saw someone commit suicide, nearly lost her 8-year-old son to illness and whose father died at 56. She would not have been blamed for thinking 'Why me? What's next? Why do the good die young?', but she consciously played winner tapes, such as 'My father had his first heart attack ten years ago, and yet lived long enough to know his grandchildren. My son survived.' As a result she was able to get through the next year a little more easily than she otherwise would have. We all know people for whom the glass always appears half full instead of half empty.

Winner tapes and customer service

While the concept of playing winner tapes can appear simplistic, choosing to view the day positively when you are a service provider is essential to providing exceptional service. When a customer uses our services and is not happy, the loser tape is 'What a stupid customer.' The winner tape is 'Great! Here's an opportunity to help the customer and perhaps he or she will buy more!'

Other examples of winner and loser tapes are:

Loser tapes	Winner tapes
There are so many customer problems.	The customer is the reason we're here.
The back room is disorganised.	How can we organise the back room?
The customer just doesn't understand.	How can we use this information to gain revenue/ credibility from educating the customer?
I have too much work to do.	Having lots to do makes time fly.

Exercise   Your winner and loser tapes. We often play loser tapes when dealing with customer problems. Write down your favourite customer service loser tapes and then replace them with winner tapes.

The benefit of using this concept within an organisation is twofold:

◆ First you will have a common vocabulary for taking a positive approach.

◆ Secondly you depersonalise the experience; instead of saying someone has a poor attitude, you say they are simply playing a loser tape. You are observing the behaviour, not criticising the person.

Sending the message

The words we use

While the actual words used represent only 7 per cent of the communication process, word choice is still something to carefully consider. Jargon, complex words and slang can all confuse the receiver, while language that is too simple can be patronising. Some important points to remember about word choice are as follows:

General guidelines:

◆ Use really specific words.

◆ Be careful with the word 'but': it tends to disqualify all other words used previously in the sentence. For instance 'I am sorry *but* we are busy' negates the apology.

◆ Use positive words such as 'we can, we will, let's'.

◆ Watch 'red flag' words. These are words or phrases that cause a negative reaction with the customer. For instance 'no, our policy is . . . it's not my job, I don't know'.

◆ Instead say 'Normally we . . . , I will find out'.

◆ Use 'we' not 'you' and 'I'.

◆ Use action words when resolving issues such as 'let's get to the bottom of this, let's work towards closure'.

◆ Don't swear and remember one person's definition of jargon could be the other's definition of swearing.

Use of humour:

◆ Be very careful when using humour with customers, particularly if there are problems or issues. Half-laughing and saying things such as 'Dear, dear, this is the third time the machine is down this week – not a good week' could escalate an already stressful customer situation into severe conflict.

- On the other hand, the use of appropriate humour can dissipate negative energy and connect disparate viewpoints. It is best to allow the customer to initiate the humour and to mirror the customer's style.
- Humour is also easier to use when there is an ongoing relationship.

When explaining/describing:
- Use strong visual words that paint a picture.
- Use analogies and metaphors to explain ideas differently.
- When giving instructions, slow down and use emphasis to clarify important words.
- Don't use too many words. Keep it simple and precise.

During the interaction:
- Be polite and respectful using words such as sir, Mrs, etc. Wait for permission to use the first name.
- Spell out names and repeat numbers.
- Consider the receiver and their fluency in English.
- Watch judgemental words such as should and ought.
- Use the customer's name two-to-three times during the interaction, particularly at important moments of truth.

When communicating policies:
- Don't use put-downs. Be as unbiased as possible.
- Never criticise other internal departments.
- Don't say 'That's not my department' but rather 'Other people specialise in that area.'

Technical terms:
- Try to avoid jargon or slang.
- If you use technical terms, make sure you define them.
- Establish common vocabulary.
- Don't make assumptions when talking to those with less technical or product knowledge.

When there are problems:
- Don't commit to solving the problem. You can commit to doing your best to solve it.

+ Don't criticise the customer or say it's their fault.
+ Express ownership when talking about problems: 'I am going to take personal responsibility for this.'
+ Be positive: 'I'm going to help you any way I can.'
+ Only provide the necessary truth. There is a tendency to tell customers everything that's happening when they only need to know what will help them to move forward in the service interactions.
+ Give reassurance such as 'looks like we are on the right track.'

Exercise   For your business, list any of the words that might confuse your customers: jargon, red-flag words, acronyms, etc.

The way we say the words

The way we say the words, or the *delivery*, has a critical impact on the extent to which the message is received accurately. Here are some guidelines to improve the delivery of your message.

+ Include some variety in pitch and inflection to add interest to the message. A monotone can cause customers to lose interest quickly!
+ Ensure your voice has good tone by using deep breathing and relaxation techniques to give it a stronger, more resonant quality.
+ The volume of your voice needs to be loud enough for people to hear, but not so loud that it dominates or intimidates. Volume can be adjusted to make important points.
+ Speaking quickly may result in the message not being received in its entirety. Speaking slowly may lose the receiver out of boredom. Slow down your rate of speech when providing important information such as detailed instructions or content facts. Quicken your speech pattern when dealing with more routine data.
+ Faulty pronunciation, including names, can result in the message not being received accurately. While the listener is trying to interpret the words, they may miss the message. Failing to articulate words clearly may also result in miscommunication. Proper enunciation means keeping your speech clear, precise and easy to listen to.

◆ We all have had habits and use filler words such as 'like, um, you know, uh,' etc. These words clutter communication and result in the receiver turning off or even counting the number of filler words we use! Either way, they are not listening anymore, so avoid filler words.
◆ Emphasise specific/important words.
◆ Use emotion to show interest and commitment.

Following are some other guidelines:
◆ Don't be condescending or judgemental.
◆ Don't sound apathetic or anxious.
◆ Don't get impatient.
◆ Be enthusiastic and encouraging.
◆ Be sincere and genuine.
◆ Do sound caring.
◆ Do sound as if you are calm and in control.
◆ Make sure there is constant dialogue.
◆ Be confident in your delivery.

Exercise

Delivery:

1. Repeat the following sentence several times: 'I did not say you stole the watch.'
2. As you repeat the sentence, place a different emphasis on each word as underlined.
3. Make a note of the different meaning you inferred from the emphasis, and why it had a different meaning.

> <u>I</u> did not say you stole the watch.
> I <u>**did not**</u> say you stole the watch.
> I did not <u>say</u> you stole the watch.
> I did not say <u>**you**</u> stole the watch.
> I did not say you <u>stole</u> the watch.
> I did not say you stole <u>the</u> watch.
> I did not say you stole the <u>watch</u>.

Answers for these interpretations are listed below.

As you can see, changing only the emphasis changed the whole meaning of the sentence. Getting upset or playing loser tapes can cause us to change our delivery, inadvertently influencing the receiver in a negative way.

Answers

Statement	Meaning
<u>I</u> did not say you stole the watch.	Someone else said you stole it.
I <u>**did not**</u> say you stole the watch.	Firm emphasis.
I did not <u>**say**</u> you stole the watch.	I implied you stole the watch.
I did not say <u>**you**</u> stole the watch.	Someone else stole the watch.
I did not say you <u>**stole**</u> the watch.	You borrowed the watch.
I did not say you stole <u>**the**</u> watch.	You stole a cheaper watch.
I did not say you stole the <u>**watch**</u>.	You stole something else.

Body language

Contrary to popular belief our word choice and delivery, as we saw earlier in this chapter, is only a small part in the effectiveness of our message. Our body language is comparatively more important. Body language is an idiom we all speak, but few actually understand. It's an extremely complex form of expression.

Body language guidelines:

♦ Body language is subconscious. We don't necessarily understand the messages we are sending. In fact, our gestures are to a large extent unconscious. How many times has someone said to you after an interaction 'You obviously did not like that person?' Our body language will often give away our true feelings, despite what we say. If we don't like someone, it will show.

♦ Body language is used to communicate attitude. How you feel on a certain day will show in your body language and in your voice. It's how you show interest. If you are playing a loser tape, the receiver will hear the lethargy in your voice and your body language will be more despondent.

♦ Body language is culturally influenced. It varies from culture to culture and what is acceptable in one culture may not be in another. Without realising this difference, we can make incorrect judgements about customers and their messages, or accidentally offend them by our own gestures. For instance, as the world watched while Neil Armstrong took the first steps on the moon, many were undoubtedly confused as to why the American was signalling 'up yours'. To many of us, a thumbs up means everything is going well, but in some parts of the world it is a derogatory symbol. In some cultures not making eye contact is a sign of respect; in western culture not making direct eye contact can be viewed as a lack of confidence or interest.

- ◆ Body language is also used to communicate power. Standing up when someone else is sitting or infringing another's space are both examples of how body language is used to exert dominance. As service providers, we must be careful not to make customers feel we are trying to exert power over them.

- ◆ When we are in harmony with customers, we subconsciously 'pace' or 'mirror' their body language. We speak at the same speed, lean towards them, nod as they nod, etc. Conversely, when we don't like a customer or are feeling defensive, we may subconsciously 'dispace' them. We may talk more slowly when they are talking quickly, we may move back or turn away. This dispacing can negatively affect the customer's experience. As service providers we can make an effort, while not appearing manipulative, to mirror the customer's pace, gestures and word choice in order to improve their perception of the customer service interaction.

- ◆ One of the most important things to remember when reading body language is that it is composed of a series of signals, not just one or two. Folding the arms combined with lifting the shoulders, putting the chin down and a severe facial expression could indicate the customer doesn't agree with what is being said. Folding the arms *only* is not necessarily a signal of disinterest: it could simply be a more comfortable position. Don't interpret only one sign since combined with other actions it could mean something else. Knowledge of body language is used to understand the way you send a message and to read the level of interest and comprehension of the customer.

Body language components:

- ◆ **Eye contact and movements.** Making direct eye contact with the customer is a way to build a relationship, though too much eye contact can be seen as dominating or intimidating. Remember that rolling the eyes will obviously not communicate a positive customer service attitude!

- **Facial expression.** Stress and emotions are often reflected in facial expressions. A smile uses more muscles than a frown, so exercise your smile!
- **Movement.** Moving around can add energy to the interaction, but too much movement in a person-to-person interaction may cause discomfort and be viewed as boredom by the customer.
- **Posture and stance.** Holding yourself upright can communicate confidence; taken to an extreme, it could denote arrogance. Don't wriggle or twitch. Don't cross your legs or lean unnecessarily. Watch barriers and move around them when you can. When a customer changes posture this is often an indication that a change in communication mode is required.
- **Space.** We each carry around our unique bubbles of space. We have three space bubbles: intimate, personal and professional. If we go into the customer's space, they will pull back and feel pressured. We can use this knowledge in two ways. First, when we want to take control of an interaction we can physically move forward. Secondly, when we want to make the other person feel comfortable we can step back.
- **Gestures.** There are over 30 gestures that can enhance the effectiveness of our message including open hands, nodding and palms up. We need to use gestures that are comfortable to us. Unacceptable gestures are pointing and beckoning.
- **Dress.** It's important to dress appropriately for the business situation. When we first meet someone our style of dress affects our credibility.
- **Breathing.** Our stress level will affect our breathing. When we are stressed our breathing becomes shallow and fast. Unconsciously, the customer can pick this up and also be affected. When you are stressed, calm your breathing; it will help you to relax and get oxygen to your brain so that you can think clearly. Be careful not to sigh if you are taking a deep breath to manage your stress.
- **Natural self.** We each possess a unique identity when interacting with a customer. It is important to assess our natural self to see how to improve its effectiveness, yet remain genuine. If we try to modify our style based on other people's styles, we'll come across as insincere. By all means watch other

techniques but adapt them to your own natural style.

Exercise	The best way to get a perspective on your body language is to videotape yourself conducting a role-play with a 'pretend' customer. Watch for the body language components discussed above.

- ◆ What were the gestures you used effectively?
- ◆ How was your posture?
- ◆ How long did you make eye contact with the customer? Were any eye movements distracting?
- ◆ How well did you mirror or pace the customer?
- ◆ What movement were you making? To what extent did it help/hinder the interaction?
- ◆ How would you describe your natural self with the customer?

Body Language on the phone

'If you see a customer without a smile, give them one of yours.'

Often individuals have to interact with customers on the phone. In this scenario it is very easy to think your body language is invisible. However, try the next exercise to see that this might not necessarily be the case.

Exercise	Smile in your voice exercise. Find someone to work with and sit back-to-back with that person. One person will act as the customer service representative who gives the standard phone greeting, either smiling or not smiling. They will record if they are smiling or not when speaking. The 'customer' will listen and write down whether or not they heard a smile. The customer service representative will repeat the greeting four or five times, sometimes smiling, sometimes not.

Write down your impressions then check with the customer service representative to see how many times you were right.

Even on the phone most people can hear a smile in the voice, either through the tone or the energy exuded. So even if customers can't see you, the chances are that they know when you are paying attention and are motivated, and when you are distracted and not interested. The statistics we quoted earlier are different if you are on the phone: 14 per cent of the message comes from the words themselves, 86 per cent is from the delivery. It is often better to wait an extra ring than answer the phone when you're distracted.

One of the oldest recommendations for those giving customer service on the phone is to 'stand up and smile' as you answer the phone.

Three styles of communication

There are three styles of communication
- aggressive
- submissive
- assertive.

Aggressive communication

Communication becomes aggressive when we stand up for our own rights in such a way that the other person's rights are violated. It's when we express thoughts, feelings and beliefs in unsuitable and inappropriate ways, even if we honestly feel our beliefs to be right.

Aggression gives us the advantage at the expense of others and often serves to degrade others. It leads to a closedown in communication.

Submissive communication

When we use submissive communication we fail to stand up for our rights or we express them in a way that allows others to easily disregard them. We are submissive when we express our thoughts, values and beliefs in an apologetic, cautious or self-effacing manner, or not express our ideas at all. We might also use long, justifying explanations, often putting ourselves down, while submitting to the wants and needs of others. It leads to win-lose communication, where neither party is satisfied.

Assertive communication

Both aggressive and submissive communication are 'automatic'. They originate from the body's fight (aggressive) or flight (submissive) response. Assertive communication is the most misunderstood: it involves standing up for our own rights, in a way that does not violate another person's. It requires a conscious and deliberate choice as it supersedes our body's natural reactions. It leads to an open and honest communication of our own point of view while at the same time showing we understand the other person's position.

For instance, if asked by the customer for something that's completely unrealistic (a fairly common occurrence!) the replies could be:

- ◆ Aggressive: 'You have got to be kidding – that's completely unrealistic!'
- ◆ Submissive: 'Well I guess we could do that, er . . . '
- ◆ Assertive: 'I understand you have some critical requirements. Let's discuss what we can do to meet your needs.'

Exercise   Aggressive, submissive and assertive communication. Write down the details of a situation when you have received an unrealistic request from a colleague or customer. List an aggressive, submissive and assertive response.

Now let's look at how each of our profiled companies approached training their people. The skills described in the curriculum will be documented in Chapter 6.

Case study: Cleanworks trains its people

Cleanworks was in the enviable position of being able to train and reinforce the best personal service skills from the start. With the funding of a major corporation, it was able to establish a model for training that it called Cleanworks University.

Cleanworks University was chartered to provide the organisation's employees with the skills and knowledge they needed to deliver exemplary service and a top-quality product. Cleanworks University provided the interface between employees and a comprehensive range of education resources including classroom courses, reference materials and self-directed learning units. Cleanworks University was not actually a building but more of a 'shop window' to allow employees to view educational offerings. It was a brokered learning facility with resources from a variety of suppliers, some internal and some external. As Cleanworks wished to use self-directed teams instead of the traditional union structure, the University also included in its curriculum training for employees on working in self-directed teams. Figure 11 shows a sample curriculum for customer service training.

The university curriculum included a curriculum for team leadership (for more

Step in process	Skills/knowledge required	Resources suggested
Orientation to culture (for all employees)	Knowledge • personal and material service • internal and external customers • moments of truth • Cleanworks brand and strategy • communication process Skills • verbal communication • non-verbal communication	Psychology of service • one day • presented by EM-Power • whole company attends in one session • every participant receives a workbook • session is interactive with exercises and group discussions
Telephone interaction techniques (for call centre staff and managers)	Knowledge • communication process • customer interaction model • telephone etiquette Skills • telephone interaction • building rapport • words to use/not to use • open-ended questions • active listening • paraphrasing • probing for specifics • generating solutions • configuration and verification • managing irate customers (CLEAR Technique)	Telephone interaction skills • two days • initially presented by EM-Power • EM-Power trains internal trainers • 12 people per session • every participant receives a workbook • session is interactive with detailed video-taped role plays • feedback after each session is fed into process improvement approach
Managing customer perceptions (for van drivers and managers)	Knowledge • communication process • customer interaction model Skills • face-to-face interaction • building rapport • words to use/not to use • open-ended questions • active listening • paraphrasing • probing for specifics • generating solutions • confirmation and verification • managing irate customers (CLEAR Technique)	Telephone interaction skills • two days • initially presented by EM-Power • EM-Power trains internal trainers • 12 people per session • every participant receives a workbook • session is interactive with detailed video-taped role plays • feedback after each session is fed into process improvement approach

Fig. 11. Sample curriculum for customer service training.

information see Chapter 10) and technical/product knowledge. The technical/ product knowledge included more computer-based training and self-paced packages. The interpersonal skills used more traditional classroom delivery methodology. Figure 12 shows a sample curriculum for technical training.

Case study: Kitchen Barn trains its people

Kitchen Barn used its internal training department as a partner in developing and rolling out customer service training. Gary decided to initiate wall-to-wall training: every person in every store would be trained, no matter how long they had worked for the company. The purpose of this approach was to ensure that all people heard the same message at the same time.

The training department had only two people so it was decided to train the District Managers to run the programme. Facilitation skills and coaching skills are remarkably similar and Gary thought that if they couldn't facilitate, maybe they shouldn't be managers.

The following approach was used to institutionalise the customer service training:

1. The Training Director drafted a preliminary training programme based on her assessment of the competencies and skills required.
2. A pilot programme was run with key store personnel including Sales Associates, District Managers and Regional Managers. The programme was used as a discussion to delete irrelevant content and insert customised case studies and situations.
3. The Training Director then redesigned the programme based on the input and ran a second pilot programme. This was again attended by a similar cross-section of different staff. The programme coined the acronym GUEST for its customer service philosophy:
   G: Greet the customer
   U: Understand customer needs
   E: Explain features and benefits
   S: Suggest additional items
   T: Thank the customer.

With the successful completion of this programme the Training Director then created a leaders' guide and visual aids so any trainer could run it.

4. She then conducted a train-the-trainer programme comprising:
   ◆ Facilitation skills training for the trainers (all 22 District Managers became trainers).
   ◆ The trainers attended the programme as participants.
   ◆ The Training Director gave the trainer's overview for each module using the leaders' guide.

Step in process	Skills/knowledge required	Resources available
Overview • dry cleaning • laundry	Knowledge • dry-cleaning cycle • laundry process	Ideas • use diversity to create a 'what is laundry' module based on process manual • use IFI materials for 'what is dry cleaning' module • include general information about Cleanworks and the process of managing laundry and dry cleaning from initial customer contact through final delivery of cleaned products • include information in employee orientation session and in an employee handbook

Arrival and sort process	Skills
	• detail orientation
	• reconciliation with consumer list
	• some communication with customer service agents with any problems
	
	Knowledge
	• of fabric types: silk, rayon, cotton, linen, polyester, wool
	• of computer data entry and system
	• of how to describe garments to differentiate them
	• of notions and trims
		Ideas
		• for information on fabric types:
		  – Neighbourhood Cleaning Association fabric book
		  – students read book
		  – on-the-job evaluation using a sample bag of laundry: ask for fabric identification
		Fabric Institute of Technology may have reference sources on fabrics
		• for computer process:
		  – Cleanworks document process and guidelines for describing garments
		  – students read process with supervisor
		  – on-the-job evaluation using a sample bag of laundry and asking inventory and itemising contents

Fig. 12. Sample curriculum for technical training

◆ Each trainer presented part of the programme, and received feedback.
◆ The group discussed in detail the challenges and learning points for each module.
◆ The trainers ran the programme for each of their stores (most District Managers had approximately 11 stores).

This approach meant that every store person could be trained in a six-week time period (over 4,500 sales associates). The programme was extremely successful and as a result it was rolled out on a one-a-year basis.

The advantages of this 'roll-down' approach are:
◆ Many people can be trained in a short time.
◆ The management team owned responsibility for the training.
◆ The management team was then able to provide follow-up coaching and reinforcement.

The possible disadvantages of this approach are:
◆ Consistent quality of all the training difficult to ensure.
◆ The District Managers could find it hard to take the time to prepare to run the programme.
◆ Fluency in the programme could be lost if training did not occur often enough.
◆ The entire management team was removed from its 'real job' for six weeks.

Case study: Internet Express trains its people

Internet Express decided to bring in consultants to train its field engineers and help desk staff. They believed that the 'outside expert' perspective was required for technical employees to really understand the importance of these interpersonal 'soft' skills. The programme was customised to the company's needs in the following way:
◆ The consultants sat in the call centre and visited customer sites with the field engineers.
◆ Based on the data collected they customised the programme to this specific market segment in the following way:
  – All exercises were geared to the company.
  – The role plays were based around TARs (technical assistance requests) that the consultant had observed.

The agenda for the programme is shown in Figure 13. _____

Managing customer perceptions	
Introduction	• facilitator welcome • ice-breaker/introductions • objectives/agenda • role of technical support
The business environment and customer service	• customer service quiz • the importance of customer service • material and personal service • internal and external customers • moments of truth
Maximising communication effectiveness	• communication exercise • understanding communication • components of communication • sending the message, communicating with the customer – role plays

Managing the customer interaction	• step one: start the interaction
	• step two: establish the customer's agenda
	• step three: establish a plan
	• step four: finish the interaction
	• video tape 'real world' role plays
	  – setting customer expectations
	  – no 'transparency'
	  – dealing assertively with customer requests
	  – communicating effectively while doing damage control
	  – handling customer conflicts

Dealing with difficult customer situations	• use the CLEAR technique:
	  – calm your emotions
	  – listen actively: content and exercise
	  – empathise with the customer: content and exercise
	  – apologise to the customer: content and exercise
	  – resolve the situation: content and exercise
	• how to respond when the process does not meet the customer's needs
	• video-taped role plays
	• feedback

Fig. 13. Sample training agenda.

Discussion points

1. How much emphasis have you placed on training your service providers with interpersonal skills? What training classes have they been sent to? How do you rate not only their awareness of their personal communication skills, but also their ability to read the customer's body language?

2. How many of your team obviously play loser tapes? How could you encourage these individuals to play winner tapes instead? How could you use the concepts of winner and loser tapes as a morale-boosting technique?

3. To what extent does communication with your customer take place on the phone or face-to-face? How does that affect the difficulty of the customer interaction?

4. To what extent do you hear your people use assertive communication? How could you support them in using assertive rather than aggressive or submissive styles?

Summary

In this chapter you have been given a comprehensive overview of the communication process and the personal service skills needed to successfully send an effective message. In the following chapter you will learn more about managing the customer interaction, before moving on to setting standards for personal service and using different skills to recover from difficult situations.

We learned the following information about personal service skills:

♦ The communication process is extremely complex and is the basis of personal service skills.

♦ Attitude plays an important role in delivering exceptional service. The concept of playing winner tapes instead of loser tapes can be used to help steer your attitude in the right direction.

♦ Sending the message effectively to the customer involves choosing the right words, using delivery to enhance the message, and being aware at all times of your body language and using it as a tool to improve rather than detract from the message. It's also clear that we can 'hear' body language over the phone.

♦ It's important to use assertive communication with customers, rather than aggressive or submissive communication. Assertive communication produces a win-win result.

♦ Organisations use many approaches to provide these skills to their employees: an internal university, a 'roll-down' training approach or the use of outside experts. The consistent factor in all approaches is customisation of the concepts to the real environment within the organisation.

CHAPTER 6

Managing the Customer Interaction

I n the last chapter we described the personal service skills involved in sending an effective message. As we stated, communication is the exchange of information between the sender and the receiver. In this chapter we will focus on the communication skills required to *successfully manage the customer interaction* and *obtain a response* from the customer.

> By setting customer expectations appropriately, we stand a better change of being able to exceed these expectations and satisfy the customer requirements.

In addition we will also briefly outline four differing styles of communication. If service providers are able to shift their style in order to match the customer's, the possibility of a positive interaction increases. Moments of truth happen when all the service skills introduced combine to create a customer impression, either positive or negative. In this chapter we will revisit moments of truth in some detail, and provide examples of specific moments of truth that the companies in our case studies faced and addressed successfully.

Managing interaction and building communication with the customer

Most of the work we have done so far has been on the way we send the message. Now let's spend some time looking at *how to manage the interaction and build effective two-way communication with the customer*. Managing the customer interaction in this way will ensure we set appropriate goals for customer expectations, and by doing so are able to exceed those expectations.

The customer interaction model to produce the BEST result has four steps:

- ◆ **B:**   Begin the customer interaction
  - – gauge mood
  - – build rapport
- ◆ **E:**   Establish the customer's agenda
  - – ask open-ended and closed questions
  - – be quiet
  - – listen actively
  - – probe for specifics
  - – paraphrase
- ◆ **S:**   Satisfy the customer's needs
  - – generate more than one option
  - – consider the customer's perspective
- ◆ **T:**   Thank the customer and verify the next step
  - – thank the customer
  - – verify who will do what by when.

Step one: Begin the customer interaction

> First impressions make a lasting impression.

What makes a lasting impression on customers is the way they are treated at the beginning of an interaction. First impressions are lasting ones. Interestingly it can take only 30 seconds to get a first impression: the body language shows disinterest, the tone of voice is lethargic, etc. We need to make sure the initial interaction is a positive, impressive one. We want customers to feel we are available to answer questions and solve problems, whether the customers are internal or external.

Not only does the first impression set the tone for the rest of the interaction, but also generally the beginning and the end are remembered more clearly than the middle – a concept called *primacy* and *recency*. By getting started in a positive way you are able to establish trust and improve communication during the entire interaction.

In this step we want to:

- ◆ Gauge the customer's mood by observing their body language in terms of facial expressions, pace, movement, etc. As you assess the customer, it is important not to pre-judge – all customers are created equally and appearances can be deceptive.

◆ Establish professional rapport with the customer by mirroring their pace, energy and word choice. For instance, if the customer is in a hurry and is speaking quickly, you need to get to the point quickly. If the customer is moving more slowly and engages you in conversation, it could appear rude if you try to move on to establishing the customer's agenda before they are ready.

◆ Rapport can also be established by conducting small-talk on either personal or professional issues. For instance you could discuss the general business situation within the company.

◆ You'll know when to move on to the next step of the interaction when the customer changes posture in some way: by picking up a pencil, leaning forward, etc. It's then time to make the transition to the most important step in managing the interaction: establishing the customer's agenda.

Step two: Establish the customer's agenda

> Don't assume.

The purpose of this step is to understand what the customer wants and/or needs. You will need to use some essential communication skills to gather the most complete information possible before jumping in to meet the customer's needs, or to resolve a situation.

The skills needed to establish the customer's agenda are:

◆ ask both open-ended and closed questions
◆ wait for the response
◆ listen actively
◆ probe for specifics
◆ paraphrase.

> It's not only the answers that count, it's the questions.

Ask open-ended questions. There are two types of questions: open-ended and closed. Open-ended questions cannot be answered by a yes or no and serve to open up communication. They are designed to gather information and data about the customer's requirements.

In our society we are not very good at asking open-ended questions since we don't want to waste time. Open-ended questions may appear to be more time-consuming initially but save time in the long run since they result in a more positive and productive interaction.

Open-ended questions begin with the words: tell me about, describe, explain, who, what, where, when, why and how. Examples are:

- Tell me about the approach that you wish to take.
- Explain what you have done previously.
- Describe the critical steps in this process.
- What is your idea?
- Why do you want to tackle the issue this way?
- Who else could we involve?
- When should we begin the project?
- Where else could we go to get help with this?
- How can we improve the existing set-up?

Exercise

Change the following closed questions to open-ended questions.
1. Have you checked the hardware in the system?
2. Do you have any questions?
3. Have you any other needs?

Answers
1. What changes have you made to the hardware in the system?
   When was the last time you checked the system hardware?
2. What questions can I answer for you?
   What other issues do you need help with?
3. What other services can I offer you today?
   What other needs do you have in terms of system performance?

> Closed questions can be answered by a yes or no and serve to gather specific data.

Closed questions normally begin with an auxiliary verb such as can, will, have and did. They are used to close down a part of the conversation and to verify actual information. Examples of closed questions are:

- Do you have any questions?

- Is that all?
- Do you want three or four?
- Will you do this?
- Have you done this before?

Either type of questions is good as long as it serves to gather relevant information or helps move the interaction in a positive way.

Remember that silence is golden.

Wait for the response. Too often when we ask open-ended questions we are either too impatient or too uncomfortable with the silence to wait for an answer. We then either answer our own questions, or ask another question, or ask the same question again. As a result the customer may get confused and become reluctant to give us the information we need. If you answer your own question, it will set the tone that you don't expect an answer.

Make sure you allow time for a response: 4–10 seconds. The time taken to respond depends on:

- The complexity of the question.
- Your relationship with the person addressed – the better you know them the quicker they will answer.
- The way the person processes data, externally or internally.
- Their fluency in English.
- Their cultural values and beliefs – some cultures are more reserved in expressing their own needs.

Exercise   Pausing:

1. Get a colleague to ask you a question.
2. Then ask them to time ten seconds and tell you when they are up.
3. How did that feel? Normally people comment that it felt more like ten minutes! Silence is not easy to manage, particularly in our western society where we value speaking above listening.

Listening is an art. Once developed, it can be priceless.

Active listening is one of the most complex communication skills yet one that receives poor attention in our society.

- At school we spent over ten years being taught how to speak, while no instruction was given on how to listen. Being seen and not heard is not the same as learning how to listen.
- Our society often places power with the speaker not the listener, so we tend to view listening as a passive activity.
- Our brains can process information at over 250 words per minute, yet we can only speak at about 125 words per minute. As a result, half the time we are listening we have time to be bored, which sometimes results in only hearing half of what is being said or not listening at all.
- Common barriers to listening include rehearsing (practising what you are going to say while the other person is talking), boredom, lack of interest and stereotyping.
- In reality, listening is an active skill that gives control of the conversation to the service provider who is listening. Good listening is a prerequisite to good customer service.

Below are a few ideas to help you improve your listening skills:
1. Pay attention to the other person. Stop your mind from wandering as they are speaking. Many people write notes while the customer speaks (in sales/telephone interactions) to help focus on the customer's words. If you take notes, write only key words. Writing the customer's words verbatim won't help your listening skills!
2. Process the information as the customer is speaking. Try to view the data from their perspective.
3. Be patient if their communication style or pacing is different from yours.
4. Don't dismiss or judge the speaker because of their appearance. Listen to what they have to say.
5. If you find yourself rehearsing, ask questions to gather more data.

Exercise   Listening:
1. Listen to the news on the radio.
2. Make notes of the key points.
3. Repeat the highlights back to a friend or another person, and let them give you feedback on how effectively you listened.

Probe for specifics

Probing for specifics is the skill of taking the basic information received, repeating it and asking further open-ended questions to gather more specific data within the subject area.

> Paraphrasing is a listening skill that can be used to clarify the meaning of a customer's statement.

Paraphrasing is rephrasing in your own words what the customer has said. Paraphrasing is particularly useful if the customer has given you a lot of complex information. It has two main benefits:

1. Paraphrasing lets the customer know you have digested the information that has been shared and allows you to correct any possible errors in your understanding.
2. Paraphrasing validates the customer's perspective by showing that you heard what was said. This can build the customer's trust and respect.

Paraphrasing is:

- ◆ Not parroting back word-for-word what the customer has just said.
- ◆ Capturing the content of the customer's message in an abbreviated format.
- ◆ Not making judgements or providing your own perspective.
- ◆ Showing that you have understood the feelings, as well as the content, of the message being expressed.
- ◆ Distilling the essence of the customer's words, paying attention to the underlying meaning.

Exercise

Establishing the customer's agenda. You need a partner for this exercise. The purpose is to practise asking open-ended questions, listening actively, paraphrasing and probing for specifics.

1. Individually, select a topic from those listed below.
2. Each person takes a turn at playing the interviewer and the interviewee.
3. The interviewer asks the interviewee which topic he/she selected.
4. The interviewer then has *two to three minutes* to ask open-ended questions (at least 5–10) and listen actively to gather information on the topic.
5. During the time, the interviewer will periodically paraphrase

back to the interviewee relevant points showing an understanding of the information gathered.

6. The interviewee then gives feedback on how the interviewer asked open-ended questions, listened actively, probed for specifics and paraphrased.

Make sure that:

◆ The interviewee responds to each question with the minimum information needed to answer (this forces the interviewer to ask more open-ended questions).

◆ The interviewee answers no to any closed questions. This raises the interviewer's awareness of any closed questions asked.

Topics
Select a topic to use in this exercise:

◆ hobby
◆ vacation
◆ major accomplishment
◆ favourite job.

The learning points from this exercise are often as follows:

◆ It is possible to ask five to ten open-ended questions in two to three minutes.

◆ Normally when we are interacting with a customer we ask fewer than five open-ended questions. Sometimes we ask none at all since we assume we know what the customer wants. And you know what they say about making assumptions – it makes an ASS of U and ME!

◆ Often we ask only closed questions even though we think we are asking open-ended questions.

◆ We need to ask questions in order to satisfy customer needs.

Step three: Satisfy the customer's needs

> People don't buy products. They buy solutions.

◆ It is always necessary to generate more than one alternative so you have a fallback plan if the first option fails. Try to generate as many solutions as possible before you go into the evaluation mode. By jumping to a solution too quickly, you may eliminate a better solution.

- Too often we react to the first problem or need without considering more long-term or proactive approaches. This can limit our effectiveness in delivering outstanding customer service. We must consider both reactive and proactive approaches to satisfying customers' needs.
- We tend to think about the best approach from our own perspective. We need to think about ideas and possibilities also from the customer's perspective.
- We have to satisfy the real customer need. Often, when the second stage of the interaction is neglected, we miss the important moments of truth in the interaction (see the examples later in the chapter) which results in not meeting the customer's real need.

Step four: Thank the customer and verify the next steps

> Thanking the customer is not the end. It's a new beginning.

Finishing the customer interaction means making sure the customer leaves with their needs satisfied and with the subsequent steps and commitments clearly defined.

At the end of the interaction we need to:

- Ensure the customer is satisfied. This is normally achieved by asking!
- Obtain commitments and a specific time-frame for future actions.
- Confirm/verify the above (remember what, who, when) by summarising the key data at the end of the interaction. Taking time in this area can ensure we start the next interaction in a positive way. Too often, the customer and the service provider leave the interaction with vastly different expectations.

Adapting to the customer's style

Another challenge in meeting customer needs is the different ways individual personalities are 'hard-wired'. As a result, what is acceptable and clear to one customer may be incoherent and completely unacceptable to another.

Using Keirsey's concepts of temperament will also enable you to more fully understand your and your customers' natural communication styles. Each of us views the world through our own set of lenses and perceptions, distorting reality to match our own mental picture. We are all unique individuals with our own complexities and idiosyncrasies, but for 25 centuries four basic patterns have been consistently and cross-culturally recognised in the human personality. *Temperament theory* is based on four themes. These sets serve as *fractals of personality*. A fractal is 'a pattern underlying seemingly random phenomena'.

> The human personality is complex and varying, but temperament reveals the underlying inborn foundation on which it is built.

In temperament theory we start with an understanding of the core themes and then examine our *basic psychological needs*, our *core values*, our *favourite talents*, our *common approaches* and *habitual worldview*. People with the same temperament share the same core needs and values. This does not mean that these people are all the same! There are wide varieties, but with strong shared needs. For example, string instruments are a family of musical instruments, but there are huge differences between a guitar and a double bass.

Once we understand our own basic patterns, it becomes much easier to make more effective choices and communicate with those customers who are different to us. Let's look at these temperaments in more detail.

- **Artisans** live one day at a time, seizing the day and all the freedom they can get. They are the natural crisis managers and performers. They are opportunistic, act in the moment and want to see the immediate, concrete, tangible result of their actions. As service providers artisans are 'fixers', solving the problem quickly and efficiently. Their main challenge is that they may not look for the root cause of a problem, and therefore may solve the same problem many times.

- **Guardians** are driven by responsibility and duty, wishing to serve and protect their loved ones. They are the pillars of society and need membership and belonging to a group. Words to describe guardians as service providers include customer-focused, reliable and concrete-results focused. Their main challenge is that they may be too honest with the customer in problem situations, telling the truth, the whole truth and nothing but the truth.

◆ **Rationals** seek knowledge and competence in all their endeavours. They seek to understand the operating principles all around them in order to create their own destiny. Words to describe rationals' roles as service providers would include efficiency-focused, strategic and abstract-problem solvers. Their main challenge is that they may be oblivious to the people issues inherent in providing exceptional service.

◆ **Idealists** are soul-searchers who are constantly on a quest for meaning and significance in their lives. They want to do something meaningful for this world and are constantly on a journey to help people develop and optimise their potential. Words to describe idealists' roles as service providers include people-focused, catalysts, and facilitators. Their main challenge may be that with their empathy, they may be unable to distance themselves from upset customer situations.

The main characteristics of each temperament are listed in the table in Figure 14.

More complete information on temperament is included in the books listed in the bibliography at the end of this book.

In order to interact effectively with the different temperaments, it is important to adapt your communication style to match theirs. The table in Figure 15 gives an overview of the way each temperament approaches each step in the communication process. Watch for these behaviours and then try to match your communication style with theirs.

Speaking all four languages can be quite a challenge. The lists below are designed to provide helpful hints on improving your 'language proficiency'.

Communicating with artisans

◆ Use short and more direct communication.
◆ Remember – less is more.
◆ Talk about concrete realities.
◆ Get to the point quickly and keep moving.
◆ Give feedback on their tactical competence.

	Characteristics
Guardian	• Responsible and want to live up to expectations • Look after the group. • Membership of a group is critical • Structured step-by-step approach to tasks and projects • Want to be useful, offer services • Respect rules and regulations • Get the right thing to the right place at the right time in the right quantity at the right price • Like security and stability • Prefer cooperation • Focus on standards and norms • Like to create and implement processes and procedures • Create contingency plans • Seek to preserve • Desire continuity • Change must be practical, proven and cautious
Artisan	• Quick-thinking • Value skill, especially in performance • In tune with their senses • Want the freedom to act according to the needs of the moment • Want to leave an impression and see immediate, tangible results from actions • Tactical competence • Risk-takers • Enjoy variety and action • Seek excitement and stimulation • Like new and fun gadgets • Take advantage of opportunities • Resourceful • Use colourful, colloquial language • Adapt naturally to current environment • Natural aesthetic sense of style
Rational	• Want to continually learn about new theories and concepts – search for knowledge • Want insights – look for the operating principles of the universe • Pride themselves on their intellectual rigour • Devise strategies • Want to create their own destiny • Critical thinkers • Value logic • Want precision and accuracy • Enjoy impersonal, objective analysis • Skill in design – think through all implications • Sceptical of what appears to be unproven data and unfounded generalisations • Seek progress and advancement of ideas • Respect intellectual competence in others and demand it of themselves

Idealist	
	• Need a sense of purpose and contribution to the 'greater good'
	• Need genuine, personal connections and relationships
	• Emphasise communication
	• Want to be valued for their uniqueness
	• Respect the individuality of others
	• Want to continually grow and reach self-actualisation
	• See the potential in everyone and in humanity – desire to help others achieve their potential
	• Empathise with others
	• Use metaphors to explain learning points
	• Tune into the authenticity of others
	• Seek unity and harmony
	• Diplomatic: build bridges between disparate views
	• Promote ethics and integrity

Fig. 14. Characteristics of the different temperaments.

- Tell them the end result required and let them go.
- Expect cynicism and stories.
- Adapt to their colloquial language.
- Use tools and hands-on experiences when explaining approaches.
- Talk about impact, end results and variety.
- Remember, they read body language very accurately so watch your body language cues.

Communicating with guardians

- Talk about what was done in the past.
- Explain using a concrete, practical implementation approach.
- Be specific about who is responsible for what in terms of roles and responsibilities.
- Explain steps sequentially, starting at the beginning and using numbering 1, 2, 3, 4, 5, etc.
- Be specific about the expected results.
- Expect questions about rules, what can be done and what cannot be done.
- Use more formal body language.
- Talk about your prior experience.
- Focus on efficiencies and process improvements.
- Provide lots of data and background information.
- Give practical examples.

Area	Rational	Idealist	Guardian	Artisan
Subjects	Abstract data: around theories and systems	Abstract data: around people and their needs	Concrete data: practical and tangible around process and results	Concrete data: practical and tangible around action
Structure	Strategic: categorised under headings	Interconnected around a central theme	Linear and sequential: 1, 1.1, 1, 2, 2.1, 2.2, 2.2a, 2.2b	Tactical and to the point: 1, 2, 3 . . .
Words	Precise language: sophisticated and elaborate words Analogies and metaphors	Global language: exagger-ation of data Analogies and metaphors	Traditional language: respectful and considered Examples from experience	Colloquial language: jargon slang, short and to the point Similes and stories
Delivery	Deliberate	Flowing and dramatic	Structured	Fast-paced
Body language gestures	Pulling ideas out of the air	Circles with hands and open gestures	Finger-pointing and chopping	Clawing with hands
Body language	May appear distant and preoccupied	May appear warm and gushing	May appear deliberate and formal	May appear casual and unprofessional
Humour	Cerebral: double meanings, of words and puns	Use personal examples and self-deprecating jokes	Dry: tongue in cheek, sarcastic	Outrageous or physical
Questioning style	Questioning of theories and competence	Questioning to find what's important to the person	Questioning to identify relevant experience	Questioning on motive
Clothes	May be status symbols or absent minded	No pattern	Dress of the group, put together, conservative	Dress for comfort or to create a distinct 'look'
Filter information based on	Is person competent and knowledgeable?	How does this person approach others?	What is this person's experience and skill set?	What's in it for the other person – have they made it happen somewhere else?
Approach	Pragmatic: get the job done, competitive	Relationship-based: what about the people?	Relationship-based: what about the people?	Pragmatic: get the job done, competitive

Fig. 15. How the different temperaments communicate.

Communicating with rationals

- Start with the big picture.
- Use precise language when explaining concepts and ideas.
- Give them an opportunity to analyse information and create new problem-solving approaches.
- Make sure of your facts and present theoretical information where possible. Don't bluff!
- Don't take any critical questioning personally.
- Recognise their intellectual competence.
- Define the end goal, but give them the freedom to develop the model.
- Talk about your expertise in a specific field.
- Use analogies to make points.
- Use the conditional language 'if this . . . then . . . '
- Always explain what and why.
- Be prepared to debate possible approaches.

Communicating with idealists

- Talk about the purpose of an approach.
- Provide them with positive, genuine feedback.
- Be authentic when communicating – they will pick up 'fake' conversation.
- Focus on the big picture and conceptual ideas.
- Use metaphors and analogies.
- Talk about the benefits to people of actions: ability to develop potential and the 'greater good'.
- Don't discount the global language and listen for the underlying meaning.
- Don't provide too much practical detail.
- Listen to their insights on people, which are usually accurate.
- Build an empathetic relationship.

Exercise   Speaking the four languages. Think of an idea you would like to communicate to a customer. Devise a communication strategy in order to express the idea so as to appeal to all four temperaments. Address the objections each temperament might have and list the benefits they would enjoy based on their profile. Then check your ideas with someone of that temperament.

We often find that we think we are speaking another language, but we are not!

Moments of truth

As we discussed in Chapter 2, moments of truth are the specific milestones in the customer interaction when the customer's judgement of the service interaction is made. They are similar to crossroads where you can take a wrong turn and create problems that you'll need to recover from later, or where you make the right decision and build a positive customer impression. By combining multiple positive moments of truth we create happy customers; multiple negative moments of truth can create unhappy customers.

As we discussed earlier, not all moments of truth are created equally; some carry greater weight than others. Using the service skills described in this chapter will help to ensure that you recognise and respond appropriately to every moment of truth.

From the customer's point of view, moments of truth that can create an impression in a technical support environment are:

◆ multiple transfers among departments
◆ long waiting time to speak to a 'live person'
◆ the company is using new processes or systems
◆ no answer to a question
◆ a known problem that hasn't been solved
◆ being frequently let down by many people in the company
◆ not being provided with the product or service wanted.

As you see, some moments of truth are related to material service (process/product issues/queue, etc), some are related to internal service (someone else letting the customer or you down), and some are related to your listening to and understanding the customer issues. No matter what the source of the moments of truth you, as the service provider, have to use professional communication skills to move on in a positive way in the interaction and meet the customer's expectations. In any one interaction there could be as many as 40 moments of truth: while we are managing one, we may miss the others and disappoint our customers.

For instance in a 'routine' technical support call the following moments of truth arose:

◆ Long queue time.
◆ New person in the position, therefore incomplete product knowledge.

- The product had repeatedly failed.
- The 'patch' that was supposed to fix the problem didn't.
- The person who had been dealing with the issue had failed to get back to the customer within the promised time frame.
- The organisation recently merged with another, and many of the development engineers left.
- The call-tracking system was out of date and overloaded.
- The sales person had oversold the product and its capabilities.

Any one of these issues alone could create a dissatisfied customer, but the conbination created multitudes of precarious moments of truth. The customer service representative felt as if he were trying to manoeuvre through a minefield!

When trying to optimise customer service it is important to:

1. Identify the most common moments of truth for the customer, based on your current business situation.
2. Help those providing customer service to script professional answers so they can appropriately address these issues.

Examples:

- Long queue time.
  - Don't ignore!
  - Don't say 'I know – I've told management but they haven't done anything about it yet!'
  - Apologise.
  - Say 'This is not the normal situation' (be careful if it is!).
  - Say 'The company has recently introduced a new product and this has generated a lot of information-gathering calls.'
  - Say 'The current version of the product is proving very popular.'
  - Say 'This time of day often has a higher call volume.'
  - Say 'Management is aware of the issue and is working on it.'
  - Then use a transition phrase to move onto the real reason the customer called: 'Let's move on to resolve the technical issues.'
- Someone else let them down.
  - Don't ignore!
  - Don't say 'Joe is hopeless that way – he never does what he says.'
  - Apologise: 'I'm sorry we haven't met your needs.'
  - Say 'I would not like to comment on someone else's actions

as I was not there at the time.'
- Say 'I will take personal responsibility for your problems.'
- Bridge to 'I am here now so can we move on . . . '
◆ You don't know the information.
- Don't bluff – body language will give you away.
- Don't say 'I don't know'.
- Say 'I don't know. However, I can find out.'
- Find the right resources.

Exercise   Moments of truth. Think about some moments of truth for your service:

◆ What changes have you made to systems recently?
◆ What organisational changes have taken place that might impact on the customer?
◆ What product/service issues do you know about?
◆ What complaints have you received recently?

List these moments of truth and pick one.

1. What do you feel you shouldn't say about this moment of truth?
2. How could you describe this situation positively to the customer?
3. What else could you do to ensure this moment of truth has a positive outcome?

Case study: Cleanworks manages its moments of truth

Cleanworks began to script the moments of truth they thought key service providers would experience. For instance, the people in the call centre could confront the following important moments of truth:

1. How can I be sure I can trust you with the key to my apartment building for pick-up and drop-off?
2. To what extent will you guarantee you will pick up and drop off my laundry and dry cleaning at the time stated?
3. What are the benefits to me of using your services rather than using my regular dry cleaner?

The team responsible for managing the service initiative, the management team and consultants, created suggested words around each of these questions, and these were included in the orientation training.

For instance, to answer question one: 'We are part of a large and reputable company. We take enormous care in hiring trustworthy people, who will adhere to our company standards in this area.'

To answer question two: 'We will guarantee we will do our best to meet your pick-up and delivery requirements. If for any reason we are unable to do so, we will commit to calling you in advance to schedule an alternative time.'

The key point to note in this answer is that the customer service representative is not guaranteeing they will always meet the required pick-up time. However they are guaranteeing to adhere to an approach, if the pick-up time cannot be met for some reason. This is an example of setting realistic customer expectations.

To answer question three: 'The benefits to you would be greater convenience and saving time in today's busy world. In addition, based on our access to new technology from our parent company, we are better able to control the quality of the end result.' The important factor to note in this reply is to keep the benefits related to what Cleanworks can provide, not knocking the competition by saying that our quality is much better than those corner shops.

Case study: Kitchen Barn manages its moments of truth

Kitchen Barn had already identified many of its difficult moments of truth, and had created a product information manual that answered many of the difficult technical questions asked. As a more mature company, they decided to invest in additional training for their people around adapting their style to meet the different customer styles. The Training Director created case studies that they used in their weekly staff meetings, where they had to recognise the customer's style and then decide how best to sell to this customer, based on their approach.

For instance, in positioning interior design to an artisan, the Sales Associates would focus on the aesthetic appeal, and unique look and feel. In positioning furniture to a guardian, they would focus on the history and credibility of the supplier, their experience in the industry and the quality of the product. In positioning products to rationals they would focus on the innovative aspects of design and the leading edge manufacturing process of the supplier. In communicating with idealists, they would focus on the benefits of a comfortable home and on providing a positive environment for interaction and entertaining. By adjusting their style, the Sales Associates found that they were receiving fewer objections, and enjoying their interactions with the customer more.

Case study: Internet Express manages its moments of truth_____

Internet Express used consultants to identify the difficult moments of truth that the team in the support centre were facing. Some of the specific moments of truth the group needed help scripting were:

- Company merged. The company had recently merged with another one, both companies had changed their names, and the cultures and service approaches of the two were very different. In addition, many of the company's original employees had decided to leave because they were uncomfortable with the new management philosophy. Often customers said things such as 'When you were . . . Inc, you were much more customer-focused', 'I heard that most of your engineers have left'. Some of the ideas to address these comments were:
  - 'We have experienced some growing pains in the transition.'
  - 'We are in the process of rebuilding and integrating the two technical support functions.'
  - 'There has been some turnover of staff which is very common in such a dynamic industry/organisation.'
  - 'We are currently integrating all our services into one location.'
  - 'I am sorry – I assure you we are diligently working to improve customer service.'
- Existing problem. There was a known bug in one specific product that had not been corrected initially. After some time the company created a patch for the bug, but had only proactively communicated this patch to the Gold Service customers. Often customers said things such as 'If you already knew about the problem, why didn't you let me know about it?' Some of the ideas to address these comments were:
  - 'We have just received a patch that resolves this issue.'
  - 'We have been testing to ensure that the patch really does resolve this specific issue.'
- Sales person oversold the product and has now been fired. Often sales people describe the product or service in over-generous terms in their enthusiasm to close a deal. In addition, based on the need to make a quota, turnover on the sales team is normally quite high. The company obviously does not want the service engineer to say 'You know sales people, they'll do anything to get a commission!' Some of the ideas to address these comments were:
  - 'Often the sales person has recommended a product/service based on your current business environment. As your business grows, the

original specifications may not be adequate to meet your needs.'

- 'It may be that your business load has changed and the requirements for your system are now different. Let's look at how we could assess your current needs.'
- 'Sales people do move around frequently as the market changes – he is no longer here. However I can find the name of the new sales person or the sales manager for you.'

The training programmes provided a valuable forum for the group to discuss appropriate answers to these 'sticky' questions. The result was that each engineer created a 'toolbox' of possible words and phrases to use to manage those difficult moments of truth effectively. Some of these ideas were transcribed and included in a FAQ manual (frequently asked questions) so they had easier access to the data in those stressful moments._____

Discussion points

1. How far do service providers control the interaction with the customer? To what extent do they use the BEST technique to manage the moments of truth effectively?

    B: How positive are they when they greet the customer at the beginning of the interaction?

    E: How many open-ended questions do they ask in ascertaining customer needs? To what extent do they assume they know the answer without asking the question first? To what extent do they paraphrase the customer's response?

    S: How often do they generate more than one solution in meeting customer needs? To what extent do they consider the best solution from the customer's perspective?

    T: How clear are they at the end of the interaction as to who has to do what by when?

2. How could you help your service providers to become more aware of their own style? How could you help them adapt their style to meet the customers' needs?

3. To what extent have you identified the moments of truth that service providers in your business face on a regular basis and scripted responses to help them deal with these issues? How could you begin or fine-tune this process?

Summary

In this chapter we have introduced a model, with skills and techniques that can be used to better manage the customer interaction and to realistically set customer expectations.

- When managing the customer interaction, service providers need to use the BEST technique.

  B: Begin the interaction in a positive way.

  E: Establish the customer's real needs by asking questions, listening and paraphrasing.

  S: Satisfy customer needs reactively and proactively.

  T: Thank the customer and verify the next steps.

- Every customer and service provider approaches the interaction differently. However, we tend to assume that other people view the world in the same way that we do. This can result in poor communication, and the customer not feeling heard or being satisfied.

- We briefly introduced the model of temperament as a tool to understand and frame human differences, so that service providers can adapt their style accordingly:

  - Artisans respond in the moment, are fast-paced and want concrete, tangible data about the product or service.
  - Guardians respond in a methodical, structured way and want data about experience, history and reputation.
  - Rationals respond by using questioning and critical analysis, and want abstract data and operating models.
  - Idealists respond to the relationship element in the interaction and want abstract data about benefits to people.

- Moments of truth are where the communication skills we have discussed are applied to create a positive impression of the company. Organisations can identify some of the critical moments of truth that their service providers might face and then help them script some possible responses for their 'customer service tool bag'.

*Effective
processes and
measurements
smooth
the moments
of truth*

CHAPTER 7

Implementing Effective Processes

A s we discussed in earlier chapters, service providers use personal service skills to capitalise on moments of truth and exceed customer expectations. However, *effective processes and procedures* provide the foundation for *smoothing or inhibiting the customer interaction*. Efficient service delivery systems appear transparent to the customer. Poor systems create those 'speed bumps' that necessitate personal intervention in order to satisfy the customer requirements.

In this chapter we will describe how to establish *effective service standards and objectives*, and then *evaluate the performance* of our service delivery processes against these standards. For more technically-based service delivery there is often a need for *service level agreements* (SLAs), therefore we will provide an overview of how to institute these within your organisation. Finally we will review how our three profiled companies approached defining their service standards and measuring the effectiveness of their systems.

Service objectives and standards

One of the most important facets in managing service excellence is to define specific service standards and objectives, and then measure and adjust performance to exceed these principles.

> If you don't know where you are going, there is a good chance that you will end up somewhere else!

There are two main criteria we use to create our target of effective service: *objectives* and *standards*. Objectives are concrete, measurable outcomes from specific projects. Standards define the minimal acceptable performance level within a specific category. Let's review each in a little more detail.

Establishing service objectives

Objectives are concrete, tangible, measurable results or outcomes that result from our efforts; they are the deliverables we produce. There will be multiple objectives for any organisation to achieve, within multiple key result areas (see Chapter 3). They tend to be more project-focused.

Effective objectives need to be SMART:

S: Specific. Does it home in on a particular performance component?

M: Measurable. What are the quantity, quality specifications, cost and revenue, etc?

A: Aligned. It is aligned with the organisation's vision/mission and the customer service strategy?

R: Results-focused. Does it lead to a tangible result?

T: Time-based. Does it have a specific due date?

Example

Incorrect:

♦ To contact five prospects by 31 January 20XX.

This is a task, and it does not tell us what the result is or why we are doing it.

Correct:

♦ To obtain one client with revenue of £XXXXX by contacting five prospects for training services, by 31 January 20XX.

You can see that this is an effective objective because it is:

Specific:	one client
Measureable:	size of revenue
Aligned:	with the vision
Results-focused:	the outcome, not what you will do to get there
Time-based:	by 31 January 20XX.

♦ In order to differentiate between objectives and tasks, ask three questions:

♦ What's the result?

♦ What's the benefit of taking this approach?

♦ Why are we doing this?

- Too often we write tasks and not objectives, because tasks are the things that we *do*. However, if there is no benefit, or result, or reason why we are doing it, it is a task and maybe one of those tasks we should not be doing at all.
- It is important to define and write down objectives for as many aspects of service delivery as we can. Research conducted on Yale students 20 years after they had graduated showed that 3 per cent were earning more money than the other 97 per cent combined. The only difference was that the 3 per cent had *written down their objectives* after graduation. There is something about writing down objectives that affirms our commitment to them, and keeps them in sight and in mind.
- The characteristic that gets missed the most when writing objectives is the T. Most people state vague terms such as 'within three months'. This is not specific enough – an actual date needs to be set. If the worst happens, and you do not succeed within the time frame, you can simply move the date!
- Sometimes it is hard to be specific when writing subjective objectives. For instance, when considering improving communication it's hard to quantify this increase. In this case standards can be used as the measurement device, eg number of meetings, speed in returning calls, customer feedback, etc.
- Within each major objective there will be short-term 'sub-objectives', normally set on a quarterly basis. Short-term objectives are usually less than three months in duration, and can often be part of another larger objective.
- Make sure you use words in your objective statements such as ensure, increase, reduce, obtain, achieve, attain, raise, etc.

Customer service objectives

Examples of sample customer service objectives are listed below:
1. To raise customer satisfaction levels, as measured by the XYZ survey, from 5.9 to 6.5 by 1 January 20XX.
2. To obtain feedback from 20 per cent of our registered customer base, on our current range of services by 1 July 20XX.
3. To reduce number of errors in order processing by 10 per cent to 5 per cent by 31 March 20XX.
4. To reduce the out of stock percentage to no more than 5 per cent of orders by 31 December 20XX.

Tasks to create objectives

The tasks we have to complete, with the specific milestones (the deadlines) can then be mapped out to achieve these service objectives. Tasks and milestones for two of the sample service objectives, that are within the Key Result Area (KRA) Customer Service, are shown below.

KRA	Objective(s)
Customer service	To reduce the number of errors in order processing by 10 per cent to 5 per cent by 31 March 20XX

Tasks and activities necessary to complete the objective:

Number	What?	Who?	When?	Completed
1	Collate errors from the last three months	SN	31 October 20XX	
2	Analyse errors and create two optional plans	JP	30 November 20XX	
3	Organise team meeting to make decision	DN	31 December 20XX	
4	Implement process improvements	ALL	1 January 20XX	
5	Monitor performance	DN	January – March 20XX	
6	Make changes as necessary	JP	31 March 20XX	

KRA	Objective(s)
Customer service	To obtain feedback from 20 per cent of our registered customer base in our current range for services by 1 July 20XX

Tasks and activities necessary to complete the objective:

Number	What?	Who?	When?	Completed
1	Update database	JK	31 January 20XX	
2	Decide 20 per cent of users that will be targeted	BA	28 February 20XX	
3	Design flyer/ questionnaire	CL	14 March 20XX	
4	Distribute questionnaire	BA	31 March 20XX	
5	Collate results	CL	31 March – 14 June 20XX	
6	Summarise results	CL	30 June 20XX	

Exercise

Creating a customer service objective with associated tasks and milestones.

1. Using the format of the tables above, write one of your customer service objectives.

2. Make sure it is SMART:
   Specific
   Measureable
   Aligned
   Results-focused
   Time-based.

3. Ask yourself the following questions to ensure you are writing objectives and not tasks:
   What's the result?
   What's the benefit?
   Why are we doing this?

4. Then complete a tasks and activities chart (dates) to achieve this.

Defining service standards

As we discussed earlier, for workload that is continuous, with no beginning and end, it can be difficult to write objectives that are specific and measurable with a specific delivery date. Areas that tend to be ongoing are communication, administration, etc. Also many of the personal service skills we discussed in Chapters 5 and 6, and the skills for resolving irate customer situations to be introduced in Chapter 8, also require standards versus concrete objectives.

Examples of standards in relation to customer service as a framework for performance could be:

- Reply to all phone calls within 24 hours.
- Reply to all e-mails within 48 hours.
- Queue times no more than 20 minutes.
- Resolve all level-one faults within 24 hours.
- Resolve all level-two faults within 48 hours.
- Always apologise at least once to irate customers.
- Use at least five open-ended questions in identifying needs.
- Paraphrase key data at least once per conversation.
- Always ensure that there is a contingency plan.

The purpose of these standards is to establish a minimum acceptable performance level. Often these standards when combined will result in an objective being achieved. For instance, if you fix all level-one problems within 24 hours and level-two problems within 48 hours, you would be well on the way to scoring high on a customer satisfaction survey. (Always assuming you have used the correct personal service skills with the customer!)

Defining the customer cycle

The next step in creating customer standards for your organisation is to track the steps in the customer experience. By doing this you can identify the standards and the processes required to smooth the interaction at these points. We briefly discussed the steps in the customer service cycle in Chapter 2 in 'Where are you now?'

For instance, when deciding to stay at a hotel the service cycle might include the following steps:

- Customer gathers data on the hotel from research on the Web, a brochure or a travel agent.
- Customer may try to book via the Web or telephone.
- Customer books and receives a confirmation.

- Customer calls for directions.
- Customer arrives outside the hotel.
- Customer checks in.
- Customer goes to the room.
- Customer tries to make a phone call/use e-mail.
- Customer calls room service.
- Customer organises and receives a wake-up call.
- Customer uses hotel bar/restaurant.
- Customer uses work-out facilities.
- Customer, during their stay, enters and leaves hotel.
- Housekeeping cleans the room.
- Customer uses room facilities: bathroom, TV, etc.
- Customer checks out.
- Customer leaves hotel.

As you can see, there are numerous opportunities to make or break the service experience! Identifying these steps, in detail, and then determining standards for them will result in a more consistent meeting of customer expectations.

Examples of standards could be:

- Customer uses work-out facilities:
  - clean towels constantly available
  - all equipment working
  - drinking water provided.
- Customer enters and leaves hotel:
  - doorman to greet every customer with a smile
  - staff to remember names of customers who stay more than three days
  - entrance lobby clean and free from litter.
- Housekeeping cleans the room:
  - every room to be cleaned by noon
  - refills to be provided every day
  - card to be left in each room for customer comments.

Exercise

Creating a set of customer service standards for your area.

1. Make a chart like the one below to recreate the steps in your customer service cycle.
2. Brainstorm, for each step, some customer service standards for areas that are ongoing and/or related to personal service delivery.
3. Make sure they have a specific frequency associated with them.

Steps in the customer service cycle	Service standards	Frequency

Defining systems required

Once we have identified the steps in the cycle and the standards for each, it is important to assess what systems and procedures can facilitate service delivery to these standards. For instance, the following service processes have been instituted in the New York Palace Hotel to produce consistent results:

◆ When bellboys show new customers to their rooms, they conduct a guided tour of the bedroom showing all 'gadgets' (and there are quite a few), and describing the services of the hotel.

◆ Instead of the do not disturb sign (that inevitably gets lost or moved), there are electronic do not disturb signs centrally controlled from the side of the bed.

◆ If housekeepers are unable to perform the nightly turn-down service because the do not disturb light is on, they will call the room and offer to return later.

◆ Nightly turndown service includes restocking the ice bucket.

◆ When calling for information about restaurants within the hotel, the names and room numbers of the customers are recorded. When customers arrive at the restaurant and give their names, it is then possible to greet them with 'You called earlier, didn't you?' (a personal service touch facilitated by a material service process).

Exercise   Evaluating your customer service delivery systems.

1. Make a chart like the one below to recreate the steps in your customer service cycle.
2. List the standards alongside each.
3. Now evaluate the current systems you use to deliver these standards: how effective are they in meeting customer needs?
4. Now also consider if there are any systems that could be added

to facilitate meeting customer needs more smoothly.

5. What systems exist that may be inhibiting service delivery: unnecessary steps in processes, redundant procedures, etc?

6. What changes will you make to your service delivery systems to exceed customer expectations?

Steps in the customer service cycle	Service standards	Systems required/present

Service level agreements (SLAs)

In organisations that are heavily dependent on internal service working effectively in order to meet external customer needs, there is often a need for service level agreements (SLAs). SLAs specify, in detail, the responsibilities of all internal departments to meet external customer needs. This section will cover:

◆ the purpose of service level agreements (SLAs)
◆ why SLAs are important
◆ the benefits of implementing SLAs
◆ the prerequisites for SLAs
◆ the critical elements in the SLA process
◆ developing SLAs
◆ major attributes of SLAs
◆ measuring performance against the SLAs
◆ reporting on SLAs.

Purpose of SLAs

The purpose of SLAs is to:

◆ Establish two-way accountability for service.
◆ Create levels of service that are negotiated and standardised.
◆ Document service levels in writing with, if applicable, penalties.
◆ Clearly define criteria for service evaluation.
◆ Provide a basis for improving customer satisfaction levels.
◆ Standardise methods for communicating service expectations.

Why are SLAs important?

It is vital that *all* groups involved in the service delivery process understand the customers' expectations/requirements and that they can meet or exceed them. An SLA is one vehicle to ensure that all groups understand the requirements of the customer and the marketplace.

Benefits of implementing SLAs

1. SLAs establish two-way accountability for service. The SLA clearly states expectations and service to be provided by each party.
2. All groups involved in service delivery negotiate, understand and mutually agree on what is required to meet the customers' requirements, so there are no surprises.
3. Service levels are documented in writing so all groups have concrete, well defined expectations and goals for service, which can be consistently repeated.
4. The criteria you and your customers use to evaluate service are also clearly defined.
5. SLAs serve as a foundation for improving service levels on a continual basis. Once you have accurately defined your current level of performance, you can set realistic goals for improving service and continually measure performance against these goals.
6. SLAs are the standard for communicating service expectations. These documents help minimise frustrations and bring clarity to a relationship. An SLA stated, 'These are the support levels our service organisation can provide, and this is how we have committed to support the customer.'

Prerequisites to SLAs

There are three prerequisites that an organisation and SLA implementers must meet before developing SLAs. These prerequisites are absolutely paramount to the success of the SLA process. The prerequisites are:

- ◆ Your company must have a service culture before your SLA process can be effective. Companies that have customer service cultures are those that truly place the customer's needs first.

One indication of a service culture is that the organisation possesses a thorough understanding of customer needs as well as customer perceptions. This requires the buy-in of *all* executive managers to the service culture concept.

♦ The SLA must be aligned with the company's vision and strategy so all the organisation's staff can understand the reason the SLA is in place and rally towards its common goals.

♦ The final prerequisite is that you must commit to the SLA process and implementation. It will not be easy but you must see it through.

The critical elements in SLAs

♦ Determine the parties involved in the process.

♦ Identify and determine the service elements to include in the SLA, such as:
  – products covered/supported
  – level of support and caller responsibilities
  – hours of coverage and operation
  – responsibilities
  – severity classifications
  – escalation procedures
  – resolution objectives
  – other organisational procedures.

Developing SLAs

There are five key points in developing SLAs:
1. Understand your customers' business needs and goals.
2. Define the SLA requirements for each group.
3. Choose the format of the SLA.
4. Establish SLA work groups to develop the SLA within set time lines.
5 Hold the meetings and develop the SLA.

Major attributes

Here are the major attributes that must be considered when developing an SLA:
1. Define the product, responsibilities and services to be provided.
2. Establish the manner in which the products and services will be delivered.

3. Establish coverage, response and resolution standards to be achieved.
4. Establish measurement criteria.
5. Establish reporting criteria.
6. Negotiate and determine cost of delivery.

Measuring performance against the SLA

You'll need to establish key performance measurements, who to report to and how to report against the SLA. When deciding what and how to measure consider the following points:

◆ The measurement must meet your customers' requirements so ensure you discuss their expectations with them. Work with your customers to establish key performance measurements that are aligned with your service delivery process. Some example performance measurements for a high-tech support centre are:
  – total calls received
  – call abandoned rate
  – response time
  – hold time
  – resolution time by problem severity
  – problem backlog by severity.

◆ When identifying the key measurements ensure they have a direct relationship to the process and that you can obtain precise information about the process performance. 'If you can't measure performance, don't bother reporting anything.'

◆ You must also decide the correct frequency of measurements. While once a month may be sufficient for some measurements, once a day may be required for others.

◆ Measuring performance without a strong link to process improvement is a waste of everyone's time.

◆ The manager must be able to specify why each measurement is needed, how it will be used and how it may be improved. For example, if the customer support centre currently logs a 30 per cent first-level call resolution rate, that means that 70 per cent affects the productivity of other employees, managers and directors. If you establish a first-level resolution of 70 per cent and measure against it, you can demonstrate that you have positively impacted the productivity of these employees as well as developing your own staff and their effectiveness.

Reporting against the SLAs

Once you have established your key measurements you then need to set up your reporting process. Four guidelines for reporting against your SLA are:

- Establish precise reporting.
- Establish frequency of reporting.
- Identify recipients of the reports.
- Establish an effective review and continuous improvement process.

- ◆ If the reports are to be truly effective they must be distributed to the correct audience and regularly reviewed by people who can have a direct influence on the success or failure of the SLA.
- ◆ Don't underestimate the value of reporting against these measurements. The whole success of the service delivery process is centred around the manager's ability to fully understand what is happening at each stage, articulate this and be able to make adjustments or process changes based on this information.
- ◆ Measurements and reports can tell managers information such as:
  - when additional operators may be required to handle incoming calls
  - the products that require a disproportionate share of support
  - which staff to reward based on good performance results
  - which staff require coaching based on poor performance results
  - what results can be used by marketing in product advertising
  - additional training classes needed
  - writing performance reviews.

Exercise   Do you need SLAs?

1. To what extent does service to the external customer depend on receiving service and support from internal departments?
   Score 10 if this is critical, 1 for somewhat important, 5 for some of the time.

2. To what extent do you receive what you need from internal customers when they say they will supply it?
Score 10 if this happens rarely, 1 for all the time, 5 for some of the time.

3. How customer-focused is your organisation?
Score 10 if completely customer-focused, 1 for product-focused, 5 for in the middle.

4. How effective are your performance measurements currently?
Mark a 10 if measurements are fairly current and accurate, 1 for no measurements, 5 for in the middle.

Now total your score.

♦ If you rated between 30 and 40: there seems to be a high need and the requisite support to implement SLAs, in which case begin the process outlined in this chapter or refer to the other publications listed in the bibliography.

♦ If you rated between 20 and 30: there seems to be a certain need and medium support to implement SLAs, in which case begin the process outlined in this chapter or refer to the other publications listed in the bibliography.

♦ If you rated under 20: there seems to be either little or inadequate support to implement SLAs. Instead, track your customer complaints closely on an ongoing basis to assess whether or not you should re-evaluate this in the future.

Case study: Cleanworks implements effective processes_____

As we discussed in earlier chapters, Cleanworks mapped out the steps in its service delivery cycle. They are (as described in Chapter 2):

♦ Solicit customer business by advertising, flyers and other promotional efforts.
♦ The customer calls the service centre to arrange pick-up of laundry/dry cleaning.
♦ The van driver picks up the laundry and dry cleaning.
♦ The laundry and dry cleaning arrives at the plant and is unloaded.
♦ The laundry and dry cleaning is processed at the plant.
♦ The laundry and dry cleaning is returned to the customer.
♦ The customer receives a bill once a month.

They focused almost entirely on defining overall standards for the service offered and then specific standards for each of the points of contact for both material and personal service. A sample is shown in Figure 16.

These general standards would then be filled in with more detail, when the

Stage in the service cycle	Material service standards	Personal service standards
Overall differentiators • National branding • Individualised customer service • Efficient delivery and distribution systems • Integrated information technology • Unparalleled cleaning and care technologies • Centralised operations	• Full service • Service open seven days a week: up to 16 hours a day • Standard turnaround within 24 hours • Free pick-up and delivery • Free phone number for customer service • Emergency hotline for immediate assistance • Convenient Internet access	• 100 per cent guaranteed • Personalised, customised service • Proactive in meeting customer needs • Simplicity of process • Minimal/professional interaction • Friendly, effective, staff • Clear customer service vision and values • Warranties
Marketing communications	• Strong brand identity • Quality flyers • Mailing list selection • Clear articulation of unique selling proposition • Consistent branding • Signage and 'look' • Wide awareness through intense communications (radio, TV, newspapers, etc) • Sampling and trail techniques	• Statement of customer service philosophy and values • Emotional buying factors emphasised such as safety, security, trust • Frequent usage incentives • Preferred customer cards • Door-to-door communications • Sponsorship of local events • Incentive programme • Special offers • Give-aways

Call centre	• Response time – one minute to answer the phone
	• Number of people in call centre
	  – Hours
	  – Numbers of people per hour to deal with peak times
	• Database to track inquiries to include:
	  – Laundry
		• Excellent interpersonal skills
		• able to articulate clearly the benefits of the service from the customer's perspective
		• Knowledgeable of the product
		• Trained in business development
		• Courteous and polite
		• Use of name at least

Stage in the service cycle	Material service standards	Personal service standards
	requirements – Household size – Other services used – Approximate amount spent on other monthly services – Rent or buy home – Own a washer and dryer • Scripts: – Asking for the sale – Gathering information • System set up to follow up after initial inquiry: – Flyer – Phone call	three times in the last interaction Knowledgeable about customer requirements with access to database information • Proficient in using the 'systems' • Doesn't sound 'busy'
Pick-up of laundry/dry cleaning	• Choice of face-to-face or anonymous pick-up • Flexible around customer's schedule • 80 per cent scheduled distribution: 20 per cent on call • Van design reinforces the brand • Availability of vans • Flexible routing of vans • Seven-day access on the telephone to call centre • Integration of IT for customer preferences and routes	• Greeting • Customer interaction skills • 'Pacing' • Ascertaining customer satisfaction: always ask 'Is everything OK?' • Courteous • Well-groomed • Convenient to customer • Regular routes enables customers to build relationships – greater customer loyalty

Stage in the service cycle	Material service standards	Personal service standards
	• 18-hour availability for pick-up, 6 am to midnight • Van arrives reliably and consistently around call times – within 15 minutes? • Professional dress	

Fig. 16.   Sample: setting standards.

company is closer to its launch. Building such a general list of standards also helped the company to isolate its original goal of 'excellent customer service' into its specific targeted, manageable components.

The organisation also recognised that it would need simple SLAs between the call centre and van drivers, and the processing plant. As the individuals in vans and the call centre had direct contact with the customer, it was important for them to have specific data to help them manage their customer expectations effectively. For instance, if there was a change in delivery time or place, the call centre needed to understand the lead-time the dispatch centre required for the vans to meet that new time. These agreements were not complex, but were established immediately to smooth the customer interaction.

Case study: Kitchen Barn implements effective processes —————————
Kitchen Barn already had specific standards for both its material and personal service delivery. The standards for personal service delivery were based on the content of the GUEST approach (described in Chapter 5) and included such things as:

◆ Every customer to be greeted within ten seconds of entering the store.
◆ Every customer to be asked at least five open-ended questions.
◆ Every customer to be offered an additional related or non-related item.

Kitchen Barn discovered, when it analysed its current business performance that, although it was gaining new customers in different markets, there was attrition from its current customer base. As we know, it costs a lot more to get business from new customers than it does to generate more business from existing customers. Gary decided he wanted to institute a new service objective which was: 'To increase sales to existing customers by 10 per cent by 1 January 20XX, from £ . . . thousand to £ . . . thousand.'

To achieve this objective he instituted a clientele programme, to encourage existing customers to return. Components of this programme included:

◆ Each Sales Associate had a clientele book.

◆ Each Sales Associate, in every store, had to add three new names a week to this clientele book. To this end, specific scripts were created to be used at check-out to ask new customers for their permission to be included in this book.

◆ Customers entered in this clientele book were also centrally recorded on a database, and received flyers once a quarter describing new offerings.

◆ Stores held special 'evenings' for clientele customers, either before sales or to show new merchandise.

As a result of this effort, sales to existing customers actually increased by 20 per cent, while new customers also continued to grow. A success all round, aided by a clear objective and specific standards.

Gary completed the SLA assessment, but decided that as the cooperation between the warehouse, the buying office and the stores was working pretty well, SLAs were not required. Often, retail organisations do not require such processes because of their innate focus on the customer.

Case study: Internet Express implements effective processes

Setting objectives

The Internet Express management team created the following objectives using the SMART criteria for the support centre:

1. Raise customer satisfaction levels with frontline support from the current level of 65 per cent to 85 per cent as measured by the monthly after-service surveys by developing and implementing a set of problem-handling and escalation procedures, by 1 April 20XX.

2. Ensure the average speed of answer (ASA) is under three minutes for each product queue, as measured by the weekly automatic call distributor (ACD) reports, by establishing and implementing a call queue monitoring, measurement, improvement and reward process, by 30 September 20XX.

3. Raise the first-call resolution rate from the current level of 60 per cent to 80 per cent as measured by the service call manager (SCM is a brand of call and problem tracking system) monthly performance reports, by re-engineering and improving the current problem handling process, by 30 September 20XX.

4. Reduce the backline support unresolved problem queue by 30 per cent, as measured by the SCM monthly performance reports, by establishing and implementing an escalation process and SLA with the development groups by 30 September 20XX.
5. Achieve a 90 per cent rating of all known solutions entered into the knowledge base (an internal database used to record and track down problems and fixes) as measured by the SCM to Primus Link Report by 1 August 20XX and to 100 per cent by 1 November 20XX.

The individual managers then met with their respective teams to further define individual SMART objectives with specific tasks and milestones to achieve them.

Defining service standards

The senior management team reviewed existing customer satisfaction surveys and talked with their customers regarding the specific support centre performance standards. From this work they developed a complete set of standards to cover the key areas of the support centre. These standards centred on three key areas:

◆ Service delivery including responsiveness to service calls and problem resolution.
◆ Service culture.
◆ People motivation and skills.

The management team then worked with their supervisors, product leads and analysts to develop the performance standards. Some examples of these are shown in Figure 17.

Service culture performance standards

The management team worked very closely with the technical phone analysts to develop these service standards in four main areas.

◆ Call handling: the teams developed a structured call handling and call feedback process to cover the beginning of the call, resolution of the call and ending the call. The calls were then randomly audited each week and a feedback summary provided. As described in Chapter 6 it included standards such as:
  − asking at least three open-ended questions
  − summarising the data at the end of the call
  − paraphrasing at regular intervals, etc.
◆ Phone time: provide efficient service to customers as measured by average weekly phone time of more than 30 hours.

- Dependability: adhere responsibly to the schedule as measured by ontime arrival and readiness to take calls, timely return from lunch and breaks and adequate notice of absence.
- Continuous improvement: capture all relevant data by logging 100 per cent of all calls into SCM and linking 75 per cent of the calls into the knowledge base. Additionally add a minimum of two known solutions to the knowledge base per week.

People motivation and skills

In this area each analyst completed the skills matrix and then developed their individual training plans in consultation with their supervisor and manager. The analysts were then measured on the number of classes completed and the skills matrix updated.

Senior analysts and analysts with specialised skills then gave technical talks on various areas of interest to the team and the usefulness of the talk was ranked by the team members.

Performance standard	Source	Standard	Measurement
Average speed of answer	ACD	Less than 3 minutes average	ACD reports
Calls abandoned	ACD	Less than 5%	ACD reports
Longest wait time in queue	ACD	5 minutes	ACD reports
% first call resolution	SCM	80%	# closed TARS with one attached called activity/total closed TARs
% problems resolved by second-level support	SCM	15%	# TARs closed/total TARs received
Backline unresolved problem queue	SCM	Monthly rolling average less than 30	SCM problem resolution reports

Fig. 17. Defining service delivery performance standards.

Service Level Agreements (SLAs)

The organisation invested in creating formalised SLAs. Teams were created from the support centre and engineering, with the support of the vice presidents of each function to negotiate and define specific agreements around fixing severity one and severity two problems.

Below is an overview of the sections contained in the SLA between the Internet Express support centre and the Backline support group.

The presence of these SLAs gave all the teams involved greater insight into the issues they faced, and smoothed the entire problem resolution process. _____

Purpose
The purpose of this document is to record the guidelines for response time, escalations, status updates and resolution goals between the Internet Express support centre and the Backline support group.

Scope
This SLA refers to the support of the Internet Express Software Product VSS Release 2.0 only. This software is a 7×24 supported product and requires response 365 days per year.

Definitions
Problems will be escalated to the Backline support group based on their severity. The following problem severity definitions have been agreed.

Severity	Definition
Severity 1	A complete system failure or the loss of more than 40 per cent capacity of the software system
Severity 2	A system interruption which impacts more than 60 per cent of the software system
Severity 3	An intermittent problem which causes minor impact
Severity 4	A minor problem such as documentation issues, minor feature updates, etc.

Escalation method
All escalations to the Backline support group from the support centre will be in the form of either a page or voicemail, depending on the severity of the problem, and the transfer of the correctly completed technical assistance requests (TARs) to the Backline support service call manager (SCM) queue.

Response times
The Backline support escalation co-ordinator will respond to the support centre product lead with acknowledgement of receipt of the escalation within the times listed below. Failure to respond within these timeframes will result in an escalation to the Backline support and support centre managers.

Severity	Escalation method	Response time
Severity 1	Page to the escalation co-ordinator	15 minutes
Severity 2	Voicemail	4 hours
Severity 3	Voicemail	2 days
Severity 4	Voicemail	5 days

Resolution objectives

Severity	Temporary fix or acceptable workaround	Permanent fix
Severity 1	90 per cent in 8 hours 100 per cent in 24 hours	3 days
Severity 2	5 days	10 days
Severity 3	15 days	30 days
Severity 4	60 days	Next release

Status updates

For severity 1 problems, status updates on progress will be provided between both groups on a two-hour basis until a temporary fix or acceptable workaround is applied, and then on a daily basis until a permanent fix is available.

For all other severity problems there will be a weekly problem status review meeting between the two groups where the following items will be discussed:

- Review of all outstanding problems.
- Assignment and tracking of actions items to drive resolution of open problems.
- Assignment and tracking of root cause analyses to prevent recurrence of any customer-base impact problems.
- Review of reports detailing performance of both groups and their record in meeting the resolution objectives.
- Review of the problem-handling process to provide a continuous improvement closed loop.

Discussion points

1. What service objectives could you define for your organisation/team/group? What specific areas would produce improvements in customer satisfaction levels? How can you ensure that the objectives are specific, measurable, aligned, results-focused and time-based?

2. What specific tasks or activities need to take place in order to make these objectives a reality? How will you prioritise between multiple objectives and tasks?

3. In what areas of your business, due to the ongoing nature of the activity, do you require service standards? How can you ensure that these service standards are accurate and meet

customer needs? What performance objectives do these standards help to meet?

4. To what extent have you mapped your service cycle and created standards for each step? What steps are hard to measure? Which steps are critical for customer satisfaction to attain?

5. What additional service processes or systems would help to achieve these standards? Which service processes appear to be hindering or slowing down service to the external customer? What can you do to manage your service delivery processes on an ongoing basis?

6. To what extent do you need SLAs in your business? How dependent are your external customers on internal departments cooperating among themselves? How supportive is the entire company culture around customer service?

7. If you do require SLAs, to what extent are these agreements documented and supported by all? What steps could you take to update or raise buy-in to these agreements? Which components are not working effectively?

Summary

In this chapter we have introduced a framework for ensuring that your processes support the delivery of service to your external customer

- ◆ We introduced the importance of setting SMART objectives that clearly specify the results that need to be achieved in certain areas. From this basis we introduced a planning methodology using tasks (things that have to be done) with associated milestones (due dates) to achieve these objectives.

- ◆ In some areas, where the nature of the tasks is repetitive or very intangible, the importance of defining service standards was outlined. These standards could be applied to other personal and material service, and could be based around the steps in the service delivery cycle. Creating these standards helps to make the concept of exceeding customer expectations more concrete.

- ◆ When these standards are clearly defined, it is often possible to add systems to help adhere to the standards and/or re-evaluate current systems that are inhibiting service delivery.

◆ In specific businesses, SLAs are required to clarify the responsibilities of each internal service support to meet external customer needs. Defining SLAs requires the input of all groups, and support from the company and senior management to make them a reality. Types of organisations that require SLAs are technical support functions, call centres, customer service departments, etc.

◆ SLAs help to accurately measure and report service performance in critical categories, and act as a management information tool. It is important that SLAs remain current, and therefore they need regular updating.

CHAPTER 8

Dealing with Customer Complaints

A s we discussed in Chapter 2, instituting continuous improvement is the fourth leg of the service delivery model. For this subject we will break down this process into short-term recovery, to be covered in this chapter, and then examine long-term process improvements in Chapter 9. We will begin by discussing how we can ensure that our customers have ways to communicate their issues to us. We will then describe recovery and its importance as a service management tool. Next we will look at how we manage short-term recovery by successfully defusing angry customers using the CLEAR technique. Using this technique, we will succeed in *calming our customers* and *obtaining relevant data* for improving both personal and material service processes.

Seeking customer complaints

The starting point for many of the continuous improvement initiatives can come from *listening and responding to customer complaints*. It is therefore necessary to ensure we provide systems to solicit regular feedback from our customers, and that we make it easy for them to complain to us. Ideas that can be implemented are:

- ◆ Suggestion boxes.
- ◆ Feedback forms at important steps in the service delivery cycle.
- ◆ Providing a customer service hotline.
- ◆ Personal interaction: either face-to-face or via the telephone.
- ◆ Publicising names of management who are available.

Examples of these systems in action are:

- ◆ 'How are we doing?' forms at a restaurant provided with the bill.
- ◆ Special phone numbers in hotels for customer service issues.
- ◆ Plaques that state 'We wish to keep you as a customer. If there is

anything that has not been to your satisfaction, please contact me . . . (name of Duty Manager).'

◆ Telephone calls after a car service to ascertain the customer's satisfaction with the service provided.

◆ Always providing addresses and names for written communication.

◆ User forums to brainstorm design ideas for new products.

For your business, think about how you currently manage complaints, and think about one additional action you could take to encourage your customers to tell you what is not working for them. This will also help you get positive feedback on what *is* working so you have the chance to reward specific star performers. It also lets you know what elements of your service provide the customer with the greatest value.

Defining recovery

Recovery is defined in the book *Service America* as 'the ability of front-line/customer-contact people to somehow make things right for the customer when they have somehow gone astray.'

Too often service providers regard customer complaints as a nuisance, take them personally, or deny all knowledge ('It's not my fault, it's the process').

> In fact, every time a customer complains they are really telling you that they want to continue to do business with you.

As you remember from the customer service quiz in Chapter 1, customers who don't care simply take their business and walk away. They don't tell *you*. But they do tell lots of other people on the way! Customers who do complain can prove to be more loyal customers, if their complaints are handled in a satisfactory way. At the same time, they can often provide you with valuable feedback on something that could be wrong with your service delivery process, thereby giving you an opportunity to change or improve a system.

Unfortunately, many opportunities are missed because the 'moments of truth' with irate customers are not managed effectively, resulting in the possible defection of a customer to another company, and the definite loss of relevant business data. In order to recover successfully, we will introduce you to the CLEAR technique that can help you manage these thorny interactions with irate customers.

You said what?

Dealing with challenging customer situations is a part of the service provider's job. During these situations, when emotions are running high, it can be very easy to say things that do not represent the correct image and objectives of the company.

> It is important that service providers manage these moments of truth without saying anything that is inappropriate, because this can colour the customer's perspective of the overall service that the company provides.

Some examples of true statements made to customers in the heat of the moment are:

- 'Oh we don't support that here!' – to a company that has just signed on for a substantial monthly service contract! What the engineer meant to say was that another group supported those products.
- 'We only have one person who knows this software in our group and she's on vacation.' This may be the truth, but there are certainly more tactful ways of stating it.
- 'This new call-tracking system is so bad I have to enter everything twice, so you'll have to repeat yourself.' Often, when internal systems are changed and users are not happy with the change, the person who suffers the most is the customer. When introducing changes it could be helpful to ensure that our internal employees are not being 'transparent' with the external customer.
- 'I'm sorry but Joe can't talk with you at the moment, he is working on a more *important* problem.' One word alone can colour the entire flavour of the message, particularly if this statement is made to a Chief Information Officer of a Fortune 500 company, as was the case with this statement.
- 'I can't get to you for another three days, you'll just have to wait.' Even if this is the case, a different way of stating the fact would be preferable.

◆ 'I can't guarantee delivery to you because the factory in Mexico is always letting us down – there's nothing that I can do!' Again, the customer is being subjected to the failures in the internal workings of the organisation. Not necessary, nor relevant.

These are just a few examples of what not to say. Many of these statements not only caused a rapid escalation in the intensity of the problem, but also provided inadequate service levels; a loss in two ways. During the next section we will give you some tips and techniques to deal with difficult situations and to paint the best picture, without telling lies.

The CLEAR technique

Understanding and practising the skills in the CLEAR technique will help you to work through even the most challenging situations. Again we have used an acronym as a tool for retention. However, remember that the steps do not always happen in sequence – life would be much easier if they did, but people are rarely logical in this process.

The steps in the CLEAR technique are

C: Calm your emotions

L: Listen actively to the customer

E: Empathise with the customer

A: Apologise/Acknowledge the customer situation

R: provide reactive and proactive Resolution.

In most situations there is a temptation to jump straight to the resolution stage. After all, the customer is upset with the situation and if you fix it, they'll be happy – right? Wrong!

Even if the problem is resolved, the customer might feel unacknowledged or unsupported in the process. Here's a story to illustrate the point. We were born in the UK, but have lived in the States for 12 years. For our first Christmas, as we had no other extended family with us in the USA, we decided to go out for Christmas Day dinner with our two children.

The following are the key points:

◆ When we arrived at the restaurant the place looked like a zoo – people dashing around, with no apparent structure to the activity.

◆ We ordered our dinner – it arrived an hour later and it was cold.

- When we asked for a hot meal, the server took away the plates. She returned a little while later with plates that had obviously been zapped in the microwave: the outside was steaming hot, the inside lukewarm and there was this delightful congealed rim on the outside of the plate!
- We asked to talk to the manager, who, when she arrived at the table, leaned over us and said, 'So, do you want a free meal?'
- Obviously we did not expect a free meal, but if she was going to offer, of course we will accept. So we had a free meal for Christmas.
- Were we then satisfied with the experience? No. Why not? We felt we had not been listened to or treated with respect. In fact the restaurant lost out two ways. Not only did they lose a customer, but they lost the money from all four dinners as well.
- We have since told *many* other people – and surprise – the restaurant chain has gone out of business. Not our work alone I'm sure, but we certainly made a contribution.

The situation could have been resolved successfully if the manager had taken the following steps.

- She needed to *calm her emotions*. Obviously she was frustrated she was working on Christmas Day: she probably had all reserve staff (who wants to work on Christmas Day after all?) and the restaurant was much busier than she expected. These factors caused her to be irate before she even heard about our problems. Our meal seemed to be the final straw for her. If she had taken some time to control her emotions, she would have been more able to assertively manage the situation.
- She then needed to *listen actively* to our description of the situation. By asking open-ended questions, listening actively and paraphrasing, she probably could have found out a little more about the importance, to us, of this Christmas dinner – questions such as 'I hear you have had some problems with your meal, tell me a little more about them', 'What other problems have you experienced?' etc. If the questions had been effective I probably would have told her not only that the meals were cold, but that this was our first Christmas away from home, and that we really had wanted to make it special by eating at this restaurant.
- She then had the opportunity to *empathise* with us. While she

could have demonstrated empathy using body language, she could also have used a couple of empathy statements, such as 'I can understand you feeling frustrated because the food was cold. It sounds as if we have really contributed to upsetting your first Christmas away from your homeland.'

♦ She could then have *apologised* to us, not using my least favourite apology from restaurants: 'I'm sorry *but* we're busy'. Of course they are busy – that's why they are called a restaurant! Rather, 'I'm sorry the food and the service has not met your expectations.'

♦ Then she could have asked me for my ideas for a suitable *resolution*: 'What would it take to meet your needs?' We probably would have said: 'A hot meal and a free dessert would be great', a lot less than the amount she actually gave.

So let's look at each of these steps in some detail.

C: Calm your emotions

The first factor you have to address when customers are irate is managing your emotional response. We can feel defensive, aggressive, impatient, annoyed, upset, to name just a few emotions. If you can manage your emotions, calming the customer and moving on to a successful ultimate resolution becomes more likely.

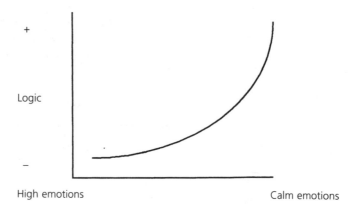

Fig. 18. Reasoning and emotion graph

As you can see from the graph in Figure 18, the more emotional you are the lower your level of logic is. Even if the resolution is the ideal, the customer won't hear it because they are still upset. Conversely, when the customer's emotions are low the logic is high, and the customer is more likely to accept the resolution.

So the first step in managing irate customers is to calm your emotions, so that you can use logic and assertive communication to resolve the situation. Some ideas that have helped calm emotions are:

◆ Take a deep breath (being careful not to exhale with a big sigh!).
◆ Mentally step back and look at the big picture.
◆ Think about the seriousness of the problem. Often problems are not as severe as they appear when we are upset. A seminar participant used the following analogy in terms of severity – was it life threatening, a permanent injury, a broken arm, a cut or a graze? Obviously these are our categories to help us put the problem into perspective – not to be told to the customer! The customer would not respond well at this stage to 'Don't worry, it's not life threatening!'
◆ Realise that the customer is not directly angry at you: they are probably angry because of the situation, or because of something else going on in their life and you just happen to be on the receiving end (the traffic was bad, the cat threw up on the carpet, their boss just moaned at them, etc).
◆ Roger Ury in *Negotiating to Yes* calls this process 'going to the balcony': not to jump off, but to put the issue in its broader context.
◆ If necessary and possible, buy yourself some time: 'I need to research this – let me call you back at 5 pm.' Then make sure you follow up at or before the time stated.

L: *Listen actively to the customer*

The next three steps in the CLEAR Technique – the L, E, A – are geared towards calming/managing the customer's emotions. Only when the customer has also calmed down is it possible to resolve the situation. In order to manage the customer's emotions, you have to be aware of what those emotions are. We do this by using active listening.

Stephen Covey in *The Seven Habits of Highly Effective People* says: 'Most people do not listen with the intent to understand; they listen with the intent to reply.'

According to Covey, there are five levels of listening:

+ ignoring the other person: not listening at all
+ pretending to listen: using yeah or uh-huh without sincerity
+ selective listening: hearing only certain parts of the conversation
+ attentive listening: paying attention to the words that are being said
+ active listening: listening with the intent to understand.

Active listening is imperative when the customer is irate. It means you listen with your ears, your eyes and your heart. You listen for content, for feeling and for meaning. You listen for behaviour, using your right and left brain, your intuition and your senses. You listen for congruence between what you hear, what you see and what you sense. You listen for the facts/content and the emotion behind the content.

Customers are explaining the impact of the problem on their business when they are talking, not when they are listening to you. As you listen to the customer, you need to identify:

+ the content or the reason why they are feeling dissatisfied with your product or service
+ the feeling or emotion they are expressing.

Example from a major airline

For instance, if I said 'I can't believe my suitcase is not on the same plane as I am.'

+ The content or the reason why I am dissatisfied is obvious: *I do not have my bag.*
+ The *feelings* or *emotions* I might be experiencing are broad and could include:

  – *worry* that I might never see the possessions in that suitcase again

  – *annoyance* over the hassle of getting the money back and filling in numerous forms in order to do so

  – *frustration* because of the inconvenience

  – *tiredness* because transatlantic flights are exhausting.

As you can see, understanding the content is the easy part: recognising the possible range of emotions is more complex. Of course this is a regular occurrence for a major airline, so to them it's no big deal: 99.9 per cent of people get their bags back – why are you upset?!' This is where the disconnect can start between the service provider and the customer.

Exercise

Active listening exercise. We will be using the same three scenarios to try out the skills introduced in the L, E, A, R. The purpose of this approach is to practise each skill, separately from the others, before you put them all together. Obviously in real life all four skills could be included in one statement, as you will see.

For each customer statement, identify both the *content* (the reason the customer is feeling dissatisfied) and the *feelings* (the range of emotions) being expressed. The answers are at the end of the section.

Customer situation 1
This is the third time you have promised delivery of these products and you have missed the dates.

Customer situation 2
I have been waiting 30 minutes and now you are telling me I am in the wrong queue and that I will have to wait again.

Customer situation 3
I can't believe you consider yourself an enterprise server company! Your system is the most unrealiable I have ever used.

In each of these situations the content, or the reason the customer is upset, is fairly easy to fix. However, if the problem is fixed without the customer feeling heard, the resolution will not be viewed as acceptable. You may have fixed the problem, but you have not fixed the customer.

Answers
Customer situation 1
Content: Missed/unrealisable shipping dates.
Feelings: Customer feels let down, doesn't know if they can trust what you say. They may also be subject to retribution inside their company for not doing their job well enough.

Customer situation 2
Content: Waiting in the wrong queue.
Feelings: Frustration, tiredness, concern that it is going to take even longer than they thought to obtain a resolution, probably feeling overloaded with work.

Customer situation 3
Content: The system is not performing to expectations. The system appears unrealiable.
Feelings: The customer is frustrated, and concerned that the system may never perform to the standard required. There may be additional concerns about coping with workload if this is the case.

E: Empathise with the customer

In active listening, we identified the content or reason the customer was dissatisfied and the emotions or feelings being expressed. Now we have to empathise with the customer. Empathy is defined as *the ability to put yourself in the other person's shoes, to understand their frame of reference*. It is not the same as sympathy. Sympathy means being involved in the other person's emotions, where you might lose the objective perspective.

In most cases it is relatively easy to feel empathy for our customers when they are upset, especially when the customer's business or personal relations are adversely effected. Reasons why customers are upset are when:

◆ their expectations were not met
◆ their expectations were unreasonable
◆ they have had an all-round bad day.

Demonstrating the feeling of empathy for the customer is important. If we are face-to-face with the customer empathy is somewhat easier to show. Using body language such as nodding, having a sympathetic expression, leaning towards the customer, etc. can all indicate concern. It is important, however, to express empathy verbally. On the phone this is obviously even more fundamental.

The way we do this is by using specific empathy statements expressed in a tone that indicates sensitivity to the customer's feelings. It is important to tell your customer directly, and sincerely, that you realise what they are going through.

Empathy technique

The technique we will use is to:

- *rephrase the content*: restate the reason the customer is upset, in your own words.
- *reflect the feeling*: put the emotions you are interpreting from the customer into words.

Example of format:
It can be . . . (feeling)   when . . . (content). (Content is the cause of the feeling.)

I can understand . . . (feeling)   when . . . (content).

Other approaches are:
1. Are you (feeling) because . . . ?
2. You seem to be saying . . .
3. It is (feeling) when (content).
4. It sounds as if you are (feeling) because (content).
5. I would be (feeling) if this happened to me.
6. I can see you are (feeling) because (content).
7. It looks like you are (feeling) because (content).

Don't just say: 'I understand'. Such a statement is a cliché. You may hear the customer say in reply 'You don't understand – you're not standing here with no bag, desperate for a change of clothes!' If you use 'I understand', make sure you include *what you understand* (the reason the customer is upset) and *the feeling you are hearing* (the emotions they are expressing).

Example from a major airline

In the airline example described in the active listening section, empathy statements could be as follows:

- 'I can understand you being disappointed (feeling is reflected) that your bags have been delayed (the content restated).'
- 'I would feel concerned (feeling is reflected) if I were missing all my favourite clothes (the content is restated).'
- 'It sounds as though you are really tired (feeling is reflected) after such a long journey (the content is restated).'

Obviously you would not use all three statements – the customer might feel that they were being ridiculed!

Exercise   Creating empathy statements. Write an *empathising statement* for each of the three customer situations we introduced earlier (see page 173), restating the *content* (the reason they are upset) and reflecting the *feelings* (the emotions they are expressing). Don't apologise yet! For these examples, as we discussed, we want to practise each skill individually before putting them all together. Obviously in the real world you would group the empathy, the apology and the resolution more closely together.

Answers

Customer situation 1

Three possible ideas (again don't use all three!) are:

◆ I can understand you're feeling *let down* (reflect the feeling) because *we have missed the shipping dates on three occasions* (restate the content).

◆ It could make you *not trust* (reflect the feeling) *any dates* we supply you with (restate the content).

◆ It must be *difficult* (reflect the feeling) to manage your other projects with such uncertainties about *delivery* (restate the content).

Customer situation 2

Three possible ideas are:

◆ I can understand you're feeling *frustrated (reflect the feeling) because* you have been waiting for 30 minutes and now you find you are in the wrong queue (restate the content).

◆ I would be *concerned* (reflect the feeling) if I thought that I would *have to repeat this process* (restate the content).

◆ I know how time-consuming it is to be *stuck on hold* while you have other work you could be doing.

Customer situation 3

Three possible ideas are:

◆ I can understand you're feeling *frustrated* (reflect the feeling) because the *system is not performing to your expectations* (restate the content).

◆ I would be *concerned* (reflect the feeling) if I thought the *reliability of the system I bought might be in question* (restate the content).

◆ It sounds as though you are *worried* (reflect the feeling) that *the system may never cope with the workload* (restate the content).

Develop your own style

One of the greatest challenges with empathy statements is making them *sound genuine*. We have to develop our own style of communicating in tense situations, showing we understand the customer's viewpoint, without sounding trite or glib. Practice makes perfect. Empathy statements are really useful in other aspects of our lives: negotiating with teenagers, reaching agreements with our significant other, etc.

Empathy bridges barriers

When you use empathy statements, you are verbally crossing to the customer's 'side' in order to demonstrate you understand their predicament. Often, when you have done this the customer then follows you back to 'your side' to resolve the issues. 'I know that is not really your fault.' Empathy statements allow both sides to *move from their positions*.

'I work for the company,' 'I need this for my job,' to instead focusing on *shared interests*: 'What do we need to do to get this problem resolved?' Empathy statements, when used effectively, are a key tool in delivering outstanding customer service.

A: Apologise to the customer

- **Don't pass the buck.** When a problem situation arises it is tempting to avoid it or to pass the buck, to say it was someone else's fault. Even when you know the problem was created by an error on the part of someone within the company, don't assign blame to any of your company's personnel. Doing so will only reflect badly on the company as a whole, and therefore on you. Apologising for the situation, without assigning blame, will help move the customer to a successful resolution of the problem.
- **Always apologise.** Often individuals are reluctant to apologise because it wasn't their fault. The point is moot – whoever's fault it was is irrelevant, you can still be sorry that the customer is disappointed with the service received. However, it is important to say more than 'I'm sorry'; this is equivalent to 'I understand' in empathy statements. It is important to make the apology specific: 'I am sorry that . . . '

When travelling with a major airline recently, we were an hour late taking off from Dallas because we had to stay on the runway waiting for a thunderstorm to clear. When we finally took off the Captain offered no apology – another dull moment of truth with an airline. When I asked the person sitting next to me about this (also a captain en route), she said 'It is not our policy to apologise for something that is not our fault.' An interesting policy. How much more pleasant it would have been to have heard an announcement from the cabin instead, 'I apologise for the delay in taking off due to the bad weather in Dallas. I will do my best to catch up some of this time on our journey.' This would not have been an admission of fault, just a politeness to smooth the journey.

◆ Don't say but. One of the largest temptations when apologising is to say 'I'm sorry, *but* the . . . ' The *but* effectively negates any words that precede it; it disqualifies the apology. The reason for the mistake often relates to internal problems and the customer does not want to know, or should not be told about these issues. The classic example is when a restaurant says 'I'm sorry your food was delayed *but* we're busy.' 'Who cares?' is my normal, non-empathetic customer response! If you want to provide an explanation, then use *however* as a bridging word, but think twice before justifying the problem.

◆ What about when the customer is in the wrong? Finally, remember the customer is always right even when they are wrong. They may not be right, but they are still the customer. You can still apologise for the inconvenience they are having with the situation even if the situation is of their own making. Take the example of a customer who has not followed the correct procedure to install a patch when upgrading a system. As a result the system failed. Obviously, if they had followed the correct procedure the system would have worked. It does not help to tell the customer that! They are probably already kicking themselves because of their mistake. It is perfectly acceptable to say 'I'm sorry the installation did not go well – let's look at how we can make it a success this time.'
The end result from the latter will be a calmer customer, more willing to work with you on the issue. When customers hear apologies it helps them calm down and move more logically to a positive problem resolution mode.

Example from a major airline

To continue the example of the lost (sorry, delayed!) baggage, a couple of appropriate apologies would have been:

♦ I'm sorry for the inconvenience the absence of your baggage is causing you.
♦ I apologise on behalf of the company for the delay in your baggage.

not:

♦ I'm sorry *but* the crew in San Francisco messed up.
♦ I'm sorry *but* most people get their baggage back at some time!

Exercise   Apologising to the customer. Using the situations discussed earlier (pages 173 and 176), write how you would word an effective apology to the customer.

Answers
Listed below are a couple of apologies for each situation:

Customer situation 1

♦ I'm sorry we have not been able to make the delivery dates promised.
♦ I apologise for the inconvenience the slipped delivery dates have caused you.

Customer situation 2

♦ I'm sorry you have had to wait.
♦ I apologise that you ended up in the wrong queue.

Customer situation 3

♦ I'm sorry the system is not currently performing to your expectations.
♦ I apologise on behalf of the company for the challenges you are facing in getting our system up to speed.

R: Resolve the situation

After you have listened actively, empathised and apologised to the customer, the emotions of both parties should be under control. Now is a good time to move the focus of the interaction to resolving the situation.

In the heat of the moment it is easy to think only of a reactive solution: one that fixes the immediate problem. While this is a good start, it is important to consider more proactive options:

◆ Is there need for a change in a process or procedure?
◆ What could be done to stop this from happening in the future?
◆ What other sources of information could be provided to customers?

Example from a major airline

To complete the airline story, the reactive solution would be to create a step-by-step plan to get the baggage to the customer, for instance:

◆ Fill in an accurate claim form.
◆ Get the address of the customer.
◆ Check in the system for any notes on the bag.
◆ Send a note through the system to discover what plane it is on.
◆ Organise the pick-up of the bag when it arrives, and dispatch it to the house.

Some of the proactive things to check could be:

◆ Was there a system mistake, which meant that the bag did not get on the same aeroplane?
◆ Why was the correct data not in the record – does this process need to be updated?
◆ The centre for dealing with information and requests in the United States only takes incoming calls – perhaps the phone system should include the ability to make outgoing calls.
◆ What other services could be offered to the customer, in the event that the process does break, to make the experience less stressful? A complete set of toiletries? Vouchers for clothes?
◆ What other information could be provided to make the process easier: a list of time frames and financial compensation for each?

How did the airline do? In reality, on a scale of 1–10, they scored about 2 on reactive service. There was no apology, no empathy. I had to call four times for updates, I had to push to discover financial compensation policies, and at the first contact (one of those fundamental moments of truth) the representative said 'The system says your bag is here: have you checked the conveyor belt?' Obviously not! I wanted to not have my suitcase at 5:30 in the morning and create a problem for this person! Arguing with the customer is never a good idea.

What about a proactive resolution? Based on the reactive score card, I would be very doubtful whether any system changes would be forthcoming.

Exercise

Creating reactive and proactive resolutions. Create both *reactive* and *proactive solutions* for the three situations on page 181.

There are complete answers for all three scenarios at the end of this section. However, a complete sample response to each customer's situation could be:

Customer situation 1
I can understand your frustration that the dates have slipped on several occasions. I apologise for the inconvenience this may have caused you. Let's look now at a realistic date for delivery of your order.

Customer situation 2
I know how annoying it can be to find yourself in the wrong queue. I'm sorry you have been inconvenienced. Let me see if I can help you with your problem.

Customer situation 3
I would be frustrated if I was relying on the system and it was unrealiable. I apologise on behalf of the company for the challenges you are facing. Let's see if we can analyse the performance issue in more detail. Tell me . . .

Answers
Creating reactive and proactive resolutions: below are examples of both solutions for the three situations. The list is by no means complete!

Customer situation 1
Reactive solutions:
◆ Talk to the people involved in giving dates.
◆ Get a new date.
◆ Ask questions about what could go wrong to prevent these dates being met.
◆ Commit to call the customer directly if the dates change.

Proactive solutions:
◆ Research what happened to the last three dates.

- Is there some change to a system that prevents slippage in dates like this from occurring?
- What new process could be introduced to ensure that the setting of dates was more accurate?

Customer situation 2

Reactive solutions:

- Go around the system and put the customer to the front of the next queue (if possible).
- Say that you can get someone in that group to call you within an hour so that they don't have to wait on the telephone.
- Fix the customer fault yourself, if you have the expertise.

Proactive solutions:

- Find out what criteria caused the customer to choose the wrong queue.
- Re-evaluate the sequencing and criteria for choosing queues and reprogramme the automatic call distributor (ACD) if necessary.
- Revisit the staffing schedule against the call flow to assess whether any changes could be made to working hours, to better meet demand.

Customer situation 3

Reactive solutions:

- Fix the problem.
- Diagnose the system in terms of load and work flow.
- Upgrade specific hardware/software.

Proactive solutions:

- Review the sales process that produced this solution for the customer.
- Re-evaluate system configuration.
- Offer training as an option.

Implementing the CLEAR technique

Using the CLEAR technique, even with lots of practice, is not as straightforward as it looks. In the pressure of the moment it is often not easy to remain calm and address the issues in a controlled way. Companies can make this process easier if they identify and train personnel how to address them.

For instance, in working with a web-based marketing company, their sales force regularly faced unhappy customers with very similar issues. Samples are shown below, grouped under the category of type of upset.

Performance: typical client comments

- 'The campaign has not performed to my specifications – I was expecting to get a certain number of leads/conversions, etc. The results were useless!'
- 'Now that you say we will change the approach because of the programme not performing adequately you are telling me I have to resubmit all that paperwork. Why can't we just make a small change?'
- 'I can't read the report – it is in HTML format – how can I see the data I really need?'

Inventory

- 'The inventory has gone, despite the fact that I returned the signed contract within two hours – can't you hold the inventory?!'

Billing

- 'I have been billed twice for the same contract.'
- 'My purchasing department wants to know why you can't sign our contract instead of us signing yours.'
- 'Why is your billing time period different from the traditional print industry?'

The group identified these difficult moments of truth and used them in two ways:

1. They used them in staff meetings to role-play what each person could say.
2. From these role-plays the team created a series of possible statements (not scripts, as we discussed in Chapter 6) to answer the issue in a calm and assertive manner.

Exercise   Identifying potential problem areas:

Step 1: List some of the issues that are causing customers to become irate with you, your team or the organisation. If you don't know them, this may be a good indicator that you need to develop more processes for tracking customer complaints.

Step 2: Identify, for these issues, how many of them your service providers have been trained to handle.

Step 3: For those that have not been discussed with the team, plan some time to create possible assertive answers for these issues.

Step 4: Question each issue with the following: 'Is there anything that could be done to avoid this in the future?'

Step 5: Move on to the next section with any issues that are remaining.

Case study: Cleanworks deals with customer complaints

Cleanworks established systems to track complaints. A few are listed below:

◆ Forms were created to record any customer complaints that came via the phone. These were to be reviewed daily by the supervisor.

◆ Forms were created for the critical steps in the laundry and dry cleaning process, so that potential problems could be identified by internal staff, not by the external customer. For instance, if there was a stain that had not come out in treatment, the form recorded this, and was sent to a customer service representative to call and explain the issue and offer alternatives.

◆ The training process included specific role-plays customised to the group so that they could practise their skills.

Case study: Kitchen Barn deals with customer complaints

Kitchen Barn set up a comprehensive system to record and track customers' complaints:

◆ All written complaints Gary reviewed personally and replied within seven business days. Even when he was travelling, his Executive Assistant knew that this was critical data for him to receive.

◆ Often he would personally call the customers with his apology, request more data and attempt to create a solution. The customers were so delighted they often forgot, or downplayed their complaint.

◆ Customer complaints in the store about products were also tracked and fed back to the product development group. This group collated the data, sent the customer a card thanking them for their comments and telling them what action had been taken.

- Sales associates role-played in staff meetings some of the difficult issues they faced around furniture and window coverings. From these role-plays a reference manual was created for the staff.
- Posters asking customers what Kitchen Barn could do to meet their needs more effectively were displayed in every store with suggestion cards. The same process was also implemented internally with awards being offered for the best ideas that became customer processes.

With constant review of complaints and Gary's active involvement, gathering the relevant data for process improvements became a way of life at Kitchen Barn, and service and sales continued to improve.

Case study: Internet Express deals with customer complaints

In the technical support area, over 90 per cent of the calls are related to problems – that's why the group exists. As we discussed in Chapter 6, the group had already made the first steps in creating a 'tool box' that included suggested scripts for difficult interactions. In addition they created new systems for tracking customer complaints and issues:

- Every rep who had dealt with an irate customer was required to complete a simple form that identified why the customer was upset and what the outcome of the discussion had been.
- These forms were fed into the continuous improvement efforts (see the next chapter).
- Managers made an effort to listen in to irate customer calls, in an effort to identify whether the cause of the tension was a product issue or if it was the way the service provider was dealing with the customer.
- This data was then integrated into the manager's coaching role. (See Chapter 10 for more information.) _____

Discussion points

1. To what extent do your people understand the CLEAR technique? How often do you review and practise this technique in staff meetings to help refine the skills?
2. To what extent have you recorded the most difficult moments of truth? Have you helped your team to create possible phrases to use in dealing with such issues? Where is this information centralised? How else could you gather this data and make it accessible to others?

3. How do you record customer complaints, both verbal and written? Who responds to complaints and in what time period? How is the customer's reaction to this response tracked? How do you evaluate the effectiveness of your complaint procedures?
4. What else could you do to encourage customers to provide you with feedback?

Summary

In this chapter you have learned about the most important steps involved in dealing with customer complaints:

- We need to make it easy for the customer to complain to us – if we do not know they are dissatisfied, we are unable to take any action.
- When we know about the problem, recovery becomes an important service management tool.
- When customers contact us, we need to be able to defuse their emotions and reach a positive resolution using the CLEAR technique. We need to:
  - calm our emotions
  - listen actively to the facts and feelings the customer is expressing
  - empathise by reflecting the feelings and restating the facts.
  - apologise no matter whose fault it was
  - move on to a positive reactive and proactive resolution.
- Even though we can teach the CLEAR technique, we have to recognise the common causes for upset customers. Once we do this we can consistently train our people so they have answers to these situations. We can then adopt a problem-solving approach to see if we can eliminate these issues in the long term.

CHAPTER 9

Instituting Continuous Improvement Processes

A s we discussed in Chapter 2, instituting continuous improvement is the fourth leg of the service delivery model. In this chapter we will investigate how we can incorporate the feedback from customer complaints into more long-term process improvements or adaptation. More often than not, we implement a reactive solution to the customer's situation, while not looking any further into the root cause of any problems. We need to ensure that we also include proactive problem resolution, to prevent upsets to future customers. In addition, constantly updating internal material processes is pivotal in exceeding customer expectations. Finally we look briefly at re-engineering and describe its role in improving customer service levels.

Long-term process improvements

Most of the time we accomplish the reactive solution successfully, but then we are unable, unwilling or too preoccupied with current events to evaluate and implement the proactive options. As a result we tend to solve the same problem again and again, but in different ways! Short-term gain produces long-term loss.

In order to ensure we are consistently improving existing processes, and solving a problem once rather than many times, it's important to use an effective *problem-solving methodology* and to constantly *question systems and procedures*.

Problem-solving

No matter how organised and structured the material service processes are, things break. We live in a rapidly changing world, and humans are more than capable of errors. Problems often occur. These can encompass major issues such as system faults, missed shipping deadlines, shortfalls in sales, communication issues such as conflicts and misunderstandings, and smaller mistakes such as wrong data entry, missed mini-milestones and mistakes. When any problem occurs, there is a tendency to react and fix it, but sometimes the symptom gets fixed, not the root cause.

> Successful problem resolution involves identifying the source of the problem and then using proactive strategies to prevent it from recurring.

Organisations which adopt these proactive problem-solving approaches will save time long-term and be more able to deliver outstanding customer service.

Proactive problem-solving involves a number of steps:
1. Perceive the problem
2. Define the problem
3. Analyse the problem
4. Generate alternatives
5. Evaluate alternatives
6. Make a decision and implement.

Figure 19 gives some ideas for questions to ask, and guidelines for approaching each step in this process. Examples of this process in action are included in the case studies later in the chapter.

Exercise   Solving a problem. Analyse a current problem that is affecting service to the customer and work through the process to identify some possible solutions. Think carefully about the underlying root cause of the problem.

1. Perceive the problem: what is it?
2. Define the problem: be specific. Make sure you find the root cause.
3. Analyse the problem: what are the components of the problem?
4. Generate alternatives: what are some possibilities, both conventional and unconventional?
5. Evaluate alternatives: what criteria will you be using to decide on a solution?
6. Make a decision and implement: who is going to do what by when?

Problem-solving step	Questions	Guidelines
Perceive the problem	• Is there a problem? • What does it look like? • Where is the problem?	• Don't assume a problem is bad • Look for the real problem

Define the problem	• What are the facets of the problem?
	• Is it a tangible problem (missing deadlines, sales targets)?
	• Is it an intangible problem (conflicts)?
		• Avoid assumptions
		• Create a problem definition that:
		  – is specific and measurable
		  – shows how the problem relates to the customer and the organisation

Analyse the problem	• What is the problem and what are the symptoms of the problem? • What is really the root cause?	• Don't jump to resolution too quickly • Use an analysis tool such as a fishbone diagram
Generate alternatives	• How could we approach this problem differently? • What are some new ideas? • What are ideas we tried once before but could adapt?	• Generate as many ideas as possible • Record all ideas • No criticising • Everyone participates • Combine and build on ideas
Evaluate alternatives	• What criteria shall we use? • How will we weight options? • How will we balance objective and subjective criteria?	• Make sure the criteria are verbalised • Listen to all team members' input • Be aware of win-lose tactics
Make a decision and implement	• To what extent is this solution satisfactory to all? • Do we have time to care?	• Try for a win-win solution • Consider other restraints such as time and resources

Fig. 19. Problem-solving questions and guidelines.

Customer service task forces

Many organisations decide, when they institute the customer service initiative, to establish customer service tasks forces. These teams play several important roles in driving up customer service levels:

- They involve a broader spectrum of people, often from diverse groups within the company.
- They are able to make recommendations and implement specific process improvements.
- They keep customer service 'in sight and in mind'.

In order for these customer service task forces to have a chance of being successful there are certain requirements:

1. Senior management must be committed to the task forces, listen to their input and empower them to make changes.
2. Each task force needs to have a trained facilitator – many such groups fail because there is no one person trained to guide the group process.
3. The task force must be allowed time to work on their allocated task. This sounds obvious, but it is amazing how many managers expect such work to be conducted above and beyond their employees' normal workload.
4. Time needs to be invested in ensuring that the right skill and experience mix is included on each task force. Being alive is not the only requirement!

With these qualifications met, the task forces can prove to be an active and effective tool in helping the company to exceed customer expectations. As we discussed in Chapter 2, the Customer First teams at British Airways played a fundamental role in instituting new systems and procedures to better meet customers' needs.

Updating SLAs

Ongoing maintenance of SLAs

An SLA needs to be a living document. Ongoing maintenance of your SLAs means the difference between a fully living and effective document that reflects how you meet your customers' needs and a document that's been forgotten in a file drawer.

They must change and develop as your customer requirements and expectations change. There must be a process in place to link the SLAs with customer satisfaction to understand when and how your customers' demands change so that you can revisit and revise your SLAs.

There are four steps to consider:

1. Conduct monthly performance reviews with customers, management and employees.
2. Conduct proactive analysis of service disruptions.
3. Renegotiate and adjust SLA reporting requirements as your business changes.
4 Establish an annual process to review and update your SLAs.

Performance review meetings

Performance review meetings are meetings that are held with key players and are a vital tool in linking your performance measurements to a continuous improvement process.

In a support centre, for instance:

- Some measurements such as an automatic call distributor (ACD) report are likely to be reviewed on a daily basis.
- Things such as problem resolution rates would be reviewed on a weekly or monthly basis.
- These reviews are usually done internally by the support group and are used as tools for the day-to-day management of the support centre. For example, if you saw a large increase in the call hold times during certain periods of the day you may want to rearrange the staff coverage to better service customers.
- The vital link between performance measurements and continuous improvement is the monthly performance review meeting with all groups involved in the service delivery process. At this meeting, all groups come prepared to present their key performance measurements for the previous month to a senior manager. At this meeting service levels and effectiveness can be reviewed, any issues raised, improvement actions assigned and progress monitored.
- If this meeting is set up and handled correctly, it can be a very powerful tool to manage internal processes.

Re-engineering service delivery

Sometimes customer complaints or a fundamental change in the way the business operates means that the entire service delivery system needs to be re-evaluated and redesigned. Such a process is currently known as re-engineering, but the approach can also be very similar to that advocated in total quality management (TQM). This subject material is beyond the scope of this book, therefore specific reference books are included in the bibliography.

Case study: Cleanworks: continuous improvement _____

Cleanworks was still not an operating business, therefore there were no improvements that could be implemented!

Case study: Kitchen Barn: continuous improvement _____

Kitchen Barn undertook a more proactive problem-solving approach with customer complaints:

◆ Customer complaints in the store about products were tracked and fed back to the product development group. This group collated the data, sent the customer a card thanking them for their comments and telling them what action had been taken.

◆ GUEST implementation teams were established in every district. Their role was to monitor the customer and employee suggestions and recommend improvements to management.

◆ One of the frequent complaints from customers was that the display shelves were awkward, the products difficult to identify and prices were not clear enough for all items. Customers were complaining when they reached the register that the products were more than they thought.

◆ At first sight this could have been a signage issue, but the GUEST team decided to use the problem-solving approach that was recommended in this book (see Figure 20).

With the success of the GUEST teams and the application of the proactive problem-solving methodology, continuous improvement became a way of life at Kitchen Barn.

Case study: Internet Express: continuous improvement _____

Problem-solving

As you know Internet Express is a high-tech computer software support centre, which was supporting over 30,000 customers covering over 50 products. Initially, Arthur advocated the problem-solving approach for his team. An example of a

Problem-solving step	Questions	Information/action
Perceive the problem	• Is there a problem? • What does it look like? • Where is the problem?	• Customers could not read the display easily • Customers were complaining that the price they were charged was not the same as the one on the display
Define the problem	• What are the facets of the problem? • Is it a tangible problem (missing deadlines, sales targets)? • Is it an intangible problem (conflicts)?	• Display shelves are a certain width • Based on that width, it was difficult to display products in an organised way • The signage often became separated from the products
Analyse the problem	• What is the problem and what are the symptoms of the problem? • What is really the root cause?	• The shelf display had always been three feet wide • This size did not work well with the newer products This size had been initiated by the founder
Generate alternatives	• How could we approach the problem differently? • What are some new ideas? • What are some ideas we tried once before that we could adapt?	• Could we change the width of the shelves? This would involve going against 20 years of tradition • It would mean asking the founder • New in-store design was created • New signage options were identified

Evaluate alternatives	• What criteria shall we use?
	• How will we weight options?
	• How will we balance objective and subjective criteria?
		• The best option was to redesign the in-store shelf space because this would:
		  – Allow more products to be displayed
		  – Ensure signage was clear
		  – Drive sales more proactively while also meeting customers' needs

Make a decision and implement	• To what extent is this solution satisfactory to all? • Do we have time to care?	• The founder was asked and he said: 'I only chose the three-foot width because that was the width they cut wood. I didn't understand why no one had changed it before, because it made no sense!' The width of the shelves was changed as part of a comprehensive store redesign

Fig. 20. Sample problem-solving steps.

problem faced between two groups is shown below.

Theresa was the manager of the group in question, the first-level support group. This is the group that takes all incoming calls.

1. Perceive the problem. The customers began complaining that the response time (time to answer the phone) was not quick enough and that problems were taking too long to fix within the first-line support group. Arthur began tracking performance data regularly, which showed the deterioration in response time, and raised the issue with Theresa. She initially believed that such issues had arisen before and that there was no need to take immediate action. As the situation continued, she realised that this time the problem was longer running than in previous times and that action should be taken.

2. Define the problem. In the short term, two problems were defined:
   ◆ On average the phone is being answered at ____ time, with ____ staff and ____ resources.
   ◆ Average time from the problem being called in, to the problem being solved has risen from three to six days. ____ customers are complaining about poor service.

3. Analyse the problem. Categories to help adequately define the problem were as follows:
   ◆ time of day
   ◆ type of calls
   ◆ time to answer the call
   ◆ type of problem
   ◆ people on site
   ◆ other tasks individuals were performing, etc.

4. Generate alternatives. Options generated initially included:
   ◆ change the phone answering process
   ◆ use voicemail more frequently
   ◆ reprogramme ACD (automatic call distributor) to allocate call flow more effectively
   ◆ create a new group to answer the phone
   ◆ reorganise the group.

In this part of the problem-solving process, the possible challenges in addressing the issues arose. Theresa was reluctant to consider the approaches that would result in the major reorganisation of her team. She believed she had built a cohesive unit and did not want to change the structure just for the sake of change. In involving Arthur's management team in generating ideas, Sharon, a manager from another group, expressed that she had a completely new idea for how the team could operate and be successful. Arthur was impressed by the possible innovative way out of the problem.

5. Evaluate alternatives. The team created a list of criteria on which to make a decision. Theresa presented a logical cause and effect analysis, which Arthur agreed with. Sharon was unable to clearly explain the rationale behind her proposed approach.

6. Make a decision and implement. As a result, the decision was made to try several short-term solutions (changing resource allocation, bringing in temporary help for paperwork, etc), implement these and then monitor for performance improvement.

   The call volume went down within a short time (it had been driven by a new product release and customers asking questions on additional features) and this short-term response was a success. This analysis prevented the team from hiring new people, always a time-consuming and expensive process, when a more short-term resolution was better.

Establishing project teams

However, as the organisation continued to re-evaluate its existing processes and procedures, Arthur became aware of the need to structure the approach to continuous improvement by establishing specific project teams.

The challenge for Arthur's team was to move from purely reactive technical support to a more proactive approach. The management team tended to be more junior, and loved the excitement and the challenge of the dynamic technical support environment. Every day was different! Unfortunately, they mistook their reactive mode for productivity, a common mistake, and as a result were not as focused on the long-term issues as they could have been.

For this reason, Arthur divided his management group into four long-term process improvement teams:

◆ measurements and metrics
◆ service level agreements
◆ product knowledge and training
◆ escalation process.

Any issues that arose in any of those areas were filtered to that team so as to centralise the information.

Re-engineering the support centre

However, as the organisation continued to re-evaluate its existing processes and procedures, Arthur became aware of longer-term needs for more drastically re-engineering the support centre.

Arthur decided, because of the relative newness of his team, to hire an external consultant to help with process design and implementation. Arthur asked the consultant to review the support delivery process with an aim to improve both external and internal customer satisfaction levels. Reviewing and re-engineering a poorly structured support centre and its systems may solve many of the support centre's problems.

The problem with the Internet Express support centre had already been perceived and there were a number of warning signs of a support centre at risk, such as:

◆ poor reputation
◆ under-staffing
◆ inconsistent processes
◆ unrealistic service levels
◆ low customer satisfaction
◆ inadequate training
◆ high burnout and turnover.

During two meetings among Arthur, his management team and the consultant it was agreed that the re-engineering effort would be broken into four phases.

1. Define the problem. The consultant carried out a detailed review of the support centre with respect to the six key areas of effective support:
   ◆ business alignment
   ◆ service culture
   ◆ operational processes
   ◆ people/motivation
   ◆ people skills
   ◆ tools and technology.

   During this phrase the consultants collected documentation from the support centre in these six key areas, completed a 'quick tour' checklist of the support centre, interviewed management, supervisors and analysts, and observed the staff in live operations. The consultant compiled the data from this review into the six key areas and their 38 supporting categories to determine an overall score for the support centre.

2. Analyse the problem. During this phase the consultants reviewed the findings from the data-gathering and defined the various weaknesses in the existing service delivery procedures. For instance, although Arthur and his team felt that they had done an excellent job in communicating the customer service strategy, when team members on the phones were asked about the slogan and direction very few could answer the question. In addition, in observing

the support centre, there were no obvious visible reminders such as posters, cards, etc.

3. Generate recommendations and implementation strategies. During this phase the consultants produced a report containing, for each problem area identified, a comprehensive list of recommendations and action ideas. This report was presented to Arthur and his team, who then prioritised implementation ideas and allocated responsibilities for different tasks. For instance, in terms of the lack of clarity of the customer service strategy to the team, the actions identified were:

   ◆ have an all-hands meeting to restate goals and objectives
   ◆ prepare presentations that could be used by managers within their groups at staff meetings
   ◆ plan staff meetings for directors with their direct reports
   ◆ produce screen-savers and posters stating the strategy.

4. Evaluate recommendations and implement decisions. During this phase, which took place three months after the initial recommendations, the consultants revisited the support centre and reassessed its service levels in comparison with the analysis they had completed in phase one._____

Discussion points

1. Based on your most difficult moments of truth, have you evaluated the extent to which there might be a root cause that could be tackled, and a core problem solved?

2. Pick one problem with which to try out the problem-solving approach. What worked? What was the most difficult step? Which was the most valuable step? What was the greatest benefit in using this approach?

3. How often do you regularly evaluate your internal systems and procedures? What questions have you created to ensure the validity of material service processes?

4. How could you establish customer service task forces to keep the momentum of the service initiative alive? Who could be included? How would you monitor their effectiveness?

5. Are there any areas in your company/group where the current systems and procedures appear to be completely outdated? How could you approach re-engineering these areas?

6. To what extent do you revisit your SLAs? How often do you meet the performance requirements specified therein?

Summary

In this chapter you have learned about the most important steps to define and ensure continuous improvement occurs, as follows:

- We need to move on to a positive reactive and proactive resolution.
- We have to recognise the common causes for upset customers. Once we do this we can consistently train our people so they have answers to these situations. We can then adopt a problem-solving approach to see if we can eliminate these issues in the long-term.
- The problem-solving approach encompasses the following steps:
    - perceive the problem
    - define the problem
    - analyse the problem
    - generate alternatives
    - evaluate alternatives
    - make a decision.
- By combining the reactive and proactive resolution of issues, we can constantly improve the service delivery processes.
- By constantly re-evaluating SLAs we are able to track our effectiveness in meeting customer needs.
- Often processes in the organisation have outlived their usefulness. In this case we may need to consider re-engineering, which is going back to zero and starting our processes and procedures from scratch.
- Project teams and task forces are a great tool for maintaining continuous improvements in our service delivery system.
- No matter how well we do initially in our drive to improve service, we are measured by the last customer experience. Continuous improvement is fundamental to delivering outstanding customer service.

CHAPTER 10

Helping Managers Become Leaders

A s we discussed in Chapter 2, managers are the driving force behind the customer service culture change. If they lead the process by 'walking the talk' then they act not only as role models, but are also critical in directing process improvements and coaching team members. They need to be both managers and leaders. They need to do the day-to-day activities with their employees as well as lead from the front. In this chapter we will explain and clarify the differences between a *manager* and a *leader*, and show the *contributions they can make as leaders* to the service initiative.

Leaders can make sure the objectives for delivering customer service are achieved by *defining specific standards* then constantly *assessing performance* against these standards. They need to develop their employees by providing *relevant, timely feedback* and *coaching* them on their current and future performances. In addition they need to *build a positive, productive team* focused on meeting customer needs. Finally leaders play a fundamental role in building a *customer-focused culture* by creating reward systems to *celebrate successes*. In the case studies you will see how each organisation customised these approaches for their managers.

Defining leadership

Leader versus boss

The leader plays a fundamental role in delivering high-quality service. When group members feel 'coached' rather than 'bossed' there is a tendency for a sense of ownership to develop, morale to increase and overall service to improve.

The leader	The boss
Coaches people	Drives people
Depends on goodwill	Depends on authority
Inspires enthusiasm	Inspires fear
Fixes the breakdowns	Fixes the blame for breakdowns
Says we	Says I
Says let's go	Says go

Adapted from H. Gordon Selfridge
Selfridge's Department Store, London

Being a Leader

Leaders must be able to lead their teams to produce exceptional service.

The characteristics of an effective customer service LEADER are:

L: Lead when necessary. Leaders lead when the team gets 'stuck' but allow other members to direct depending on the work the team is doing.

E: Engage the team. Leaders need to facilitate interaction within the team. Using communication skills such as open-ended questioning, careful listening and paraphrasing team members' contributions will ensure an environment where team members are heard and thus want to be involved.

A: Attitude of 'we' not 'I'. Leading means that ego has to be left at the door. A leader must be willing to allow every team member to share in rewards and recognition. If a leader takes credit for someone else's contribution or appears to be out for his/her own good, team members will become demotivated and service to the customer will decrease.

D: Do real work on the team. There are many leadership tasks critical to ensuring the delivery of service to the customer, such as organising logistics, lobbying for resources, communicating to the organisation about the team's activities and removing obstacles from the team's path. Also the leader needs to regularly interact directly with the customer. Providing this service keeps the leader in touch with customer needs and builds his/her credibility with the team.

E: Excite the team. If the leader can reinforce the team values, provide rewards for exceptional service and establish a positive environment, service providers are more likely to 'go the extra mile' to meet customer needs.

R: Results-focused. The leader plays a fundamental role in setting SMART objectives, establishing service standards and measuring progress towards objectives.

Characteristics for leaders

The critical characteristics for leaders fall into three categories:

- achieving the objective
- developing the individuals
- building the team.

Leaders help the team to achieve the objective by focusing on results and by doing 'real work' themselves. Leaders build the team by leading only when necessary and engaging the team throughout the stages of team development. Leaders also develop the individuals on the team by getting the whole team energised with their charisma and inclusive attitude of 'we' not 'I'. A careful examination of each of these areas will build an understanding of how leaders drive the customer service improvement process (see Figure 21).

Customer service leader

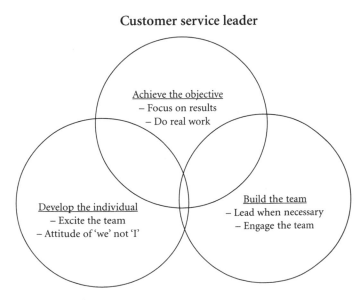

Fig. 21. How leaders drive customer service improvements.

Achieve the objectives: focus on results

The leader plays an important role in helping to achieve customer service goals in two main arenas. First, the leader defines specific objectives, sets customer service standards, and measures and monitors results. In this way the leader charts and checks the course to reaching the expected results. Much of this was discussed in Chapter 7. Secondly, the leader is responsible for many 'behind the scenes' actions needed to remove the barriers to delivering exceptional service.

One of the more subtle aspects of this role is serving as the link between the organisation and the team. This link spans several areas that include helping to reduce or eliminate barriers to customer service, ensuring the team has the resources it needs to perform effectively, and acting as the main communication channel between the team and the rest of the organisation and its customers.

Managers can undertake a wide range of activities to ensure their people can exceed customer expectations. These activities can include:

◆ obtaining access to resources (update hardware, software, improve phone system, etc)
◆ making sure service providers have the information they need
◆ negotiating with other organisational teams
◆ intervening when material service delivery processes are inhibiting personal service
◆ sifting through 'organisational politics'.

Creating the right environment is a crucial part of the 'real work' the leader must do, so that results can be produced.

Exercise

Think about the current challenges your team faces in delivering outstanding customer service. Factors could be lack of resources, problems with systems, etc. Make a list of them.

Now brainstorm actions you could take to reduce or eliminate some of these factors and write them down next to each of the factors inhibiting service delivery. Be prepared to share the list with your team members for feedback and ideas.

Develop the individual

As we discussed in Chapter 4, building the correct skill mix is significant for providing exceptional service. However, once the service providers are hired, the constant monitoring of talent and developing of individuals become paramount. For consistent managing of moments of truth, the leader must give constant feedback and ensure that team members feel motivated. By getting team members excited about what they are there to do and coaching their performance with proper feedback, the leader unleashes the hidden abilities of his/her people.

Feedback

Feedback is any kind of attention you can get from or give to another person. It is a fundamental human need and is essential for a relaxed and happy life. When providing customer service, feedback is a crucial part of improving results, building self-esteem and enhancing trust. There are various types of feedback (see Figure 22):

- positive
- developmental
- negative
- zero.

Research has shown that on average we receive six to nine pieces of negative/developmental feedback in exchange for one positive. Not a healthy balance!

Type of feedback	Definition	Examples
Positive feedback	Telling someone what they have done right normally makes them feel happy and useful by boosting spirits and generating enthusiasm.	• Praise • Thanks • Attention • Interest • Admiration
Developmental feedback	This is used when individuals need to improve in a specific area. It is given so that a service provider can take negative behaviour and turn it into positive behaviour.	• 'Next time you may want to ask a few more open-ended questions to more clearly define customer needs.' • 'You tended to speak

	The feedback focuses on the behaviour, not the person 'Go for the ball not the player!' This is the most difficult feedback to provide in a positive way.	over the customer – this might result in the customer feeling switched off. Another approach might be to . . .'
Negative feedback	This type of feedback tends to hurt or denigrate, and can make individuals feel as if they have failed, rather than learning from an experience. Negative feedback is one of the worst types of input because it actually lowers self-esteem.	• 'What did you do that for?' • 'That was really stupid.' • 'I told you not to interrupt the customer.' • 'You did . . . wrong.'
Zero feedback	This is simply the lack of any kind of feedback, positive or negative. This is worse than negative input. With zero feedback the individual is constantly uncertain of where they stand. They feel insecure, unappreciated and unclear about what is expected of them.	• Not dealing with a bad situation/action. • Not recognising someone's contribution of a good idea. • Not noticing when someone deals well with a customer • 'Blowing off' one-on-one meetings with team members. • Not providing accurate and timely performance reviews

Fig. 22. The different types of feedback.

Feedback is also given and received in many different ways:

◆ physically

◆ mentally

◆ conditionally

◆ unconditionally.

Type of feedback	Examples	Guidelines
Physical feedback	Physical feedback involves some sort of physical contact such as a pat on the back or a handshake.	In today's business climate we must be careful about the type of physical feedback we give. A handshake is practically the only acceptable form of touch.
Mental feedback	Mental feedback can be either verbal, i.e. praise or thanks, or non-verbal, i.e. nodding or smiling.	Don't forget that if you say one thing, 'good job', but your body language says another 'I can't be bothered with this' – individuals will believe the latter!
Conditional feedback	◆ Holiday, parties ◆ Bonuses ◆ Salary increases ◆ Performance appraisals	This is input that is expected and planned. It comes in response to special occasions or performances.
Unconditional feedback	◆ Verbal recognition in front of the team. with no prior notice ◆ Positive feedback from someone outside the team ◆ Customer letters of appreciation ◆ Surprise 'night on the town' award	Unconditional feedback is usually more fun and appreciated more, as it comes as a surprise. As a result, unconditional feedback is an effective way of raising individual self-esteem and raising motivation of the team as a whole.

Fig. 23. Giving and receiving feedback.

Exercise Conduct a feedback assessment for your group. Individually, think of the last few times you have given feedback to your team members.

1. *What type* of feedback did you give (positive, developmental, negative, zero)?
2. *How* was it given (physical/mental)?
3. *In what way* was it given (conditional/unconditional)?

Give specific examples such as: 'I gave positive, mental,

unconditional feedback today when I told Joe that the production of a current accurate failure analysis report was an important first step to defining the quality issues that are lowering customer service levels.' Give three examples of your own.

Many researchers have compared the effect of feedback with a bank's debit and credit balance. If service providers have a credit balance of feedback, they probably feel positive or energised. If they have a debit balance, they are more likely to feel less motivated and depressed. The positive feedback balance is an essential component in ensuring that service providers remain motivated.

Individual coaching principles

When meeting with your team members to provide feedback it is important to prepare the coaching session in advance to ensure you achieve a balance between positive and developmental feedback. Following are some guidelines to optimise a coaching session:

1. Think about the person you are meeting with.
2. Think about the area you wish to address. Be specific about the details in terms of either the positive behaviour and/or the behaviour you wish to improve. Ensure you have adequate support data.
3. Think about balancing the good news and the bad news to ensure the team member's self-esteem is protected.
4. What are the benefits of continuing or using the new behaviour?
5. Think about how the person might react and what type of questions they might ask.

Use the following checklist to guide you through the coaching process.

Coaching steps

1. Start with a positive
2. Agree on agenda
3. Get team member's input:
    ◆ Skills being handled well

Type of feedback	Steps	Guidelines
Positive	1. State the specific achievement 2. State how the achievement affects customer service, the task, group or organisation 3. Acknowledge the achievement	• Express your praise spontaneously when you see something going well • Avoid clichés such as 'good job' • Ensure the feedback is timely • Give positive feedback both privately and publicly • Use positive feedback with your team manager • Encourage the individual to acknowledge that they did a good job • Be genuine and recognise specific skills
Developmental	1. State the specific problem 2. State how the problem affects customer service, the task, group or organisation 3. Request that the person solve the problem	• Always give developmental feedback privately • Ensure the feedback is timely • Give specific positive feedback, then target one situation for developmental feedback • Only give feedback on things of which you have first-hand knowledge • Only give feedback about present behaviour, not past mistakes • Listen to how the person feels about the situation • Remove barriers to listening, such as interruptions, jumping to conclusions, passing judgement, offering advice and attempting to solve the problem prematurely • Use 'I' statements such as 'I feel, I believe' rather than 'you' statements such as 'you did . . .' • Support actions taken and follow up with more feedback.

Fig. 24. Guidelines to giving feedback.

- ◆ Skills needing improvement
4. Give your feedback:
    - ◆ Skills being handled well
    - ◆ Skills needing improvement
5. Develop action plan together
6. Confirm actions and checkpoints

You will see in the case studies the tools the managers developed to coach their teams more effectively in the service delivery process.

Motivating individuals

Motivation is a key factor in delivering top-quality service: a positive atmosphere and appreciative rewards are needed to encourage performance. Herzberg's motivation theory differentiates between 'motivators' and 'satisfiers'. Motivators are factors that inspire and motivate team members. Motivators include:

- ◆ accomplishment and achievement
- ◆ feedback
- ◆ job enrichment and growth
- ◆ teamwork.

Employees expect satisfiers to be present. If they aren't, employees may be dissatisfied with their work environment. However, since they are expected, the presence of satisfiers does not motivate employees. Satisfiers include:

- ◆ proper working conditions
- ◆ company policy
- ◆ personal stability
- ◆ compensation and fringe benefits.

Salary can fit in either category depending on the individual. Therefore, in order to effectively motivate team members to meet customer needs, leaders must offer motivators and ensure satisfiers. Providing service providers with new skills and knowledge, new challenges and diversity in job assignments will contribute to keeping motivation levels high.

Team member	Action on which to provide feedback	What to say	Ways to motivate Satisfiers to provide

Exercise Think of ways to develop the individuals on your team so they can provide better service.

1. Make a chart using the headings shown below.

2. List your team members' names in the left column.
3. In the next column list the actions on which you want to provide feedback. Make sure the actions include 50–50 positive and developmental feedback.
4. Plan what you will say to deliver the message to each team member.
5. Note for yourself which type of feedback you find easier to give: positive or developmental.
6. List for each person one technique you could use to motivate them and one satisfier you might be able to provide.

Building the team

According to Katzenbach and Smith in their bestseller *The Wisdom of Teams*: 'A team is a *small number of people* with *complementary skills* who are committed to a *common purpose, performance goals*, and *approach*, for which they hold themselves *mutually accountable*.'

Teams that have maximised their SCORE when providing service have been found to contain the following characteristics:

S: *Cohesive strategy and direction* (see Chapter 3):

- A customer service strategy aligned with the company vision and mission.
- Clearly articulated values and ground rules for providing service.
- An understanding of risks and opportunities facing the team in delivering service.
- A clear categorisation of key result areas, particularly in relation to customer service.

C: *Clear roles and responsibilities*:

- Clear definition of team members' roles and responsibilities.
- The team's responsibility is shared by all members.
- Specific and measurable objectives to measure individual results (see Chapter 7).

O: *Open and honest communications*:

- Respect for individual differences.
- An open and non-judgemental communication environment among team members.

R: *Rapid response to change*:

- A rapid response to the customers' needs as well as internal problems (see Chapter 9).
- An ability to manage and respond to change in the internal and external environment.

E: *Effective leadership*:

- A team leader who is able to help service providers achieve the task, develop individuals and build the team.

Exercise

What is your team SCORE in delivering exceptional service?

Step 1   Review the questions in each section and indicate to what extent, for each category, you are meeting the prerequisites for a customer-focused team.
1 = very clear/successful 10 = not clear at all/not successful

Step 2   Ask the rest of the team, individually, to also rate each characteristic in the same manner.

Step 3   Create an average for the specific elements. Discuss each one in turn and identify why individuals have rated them in that way and what could be done to improve each rating.

Step 4   Discuss any marked differences in rankings. For instance, if one person rated open, honest communication as a nine and another as a two, discuss the reasons for the disparity.

How easy will it be for your team to raise the SCORE in delivering outstanding customer service?

Rating: 1   = very clear/successful
            10   = not clear/not successful

Characteristic	Rating
Cohesive **S**trategy and direction • To what extent is your customer service strategy in alignment with the corporate vision and mission? • To what extent can everyone in your team repeat your customer service mantra? • To what extent is your team adhering to its values? *Overall rating in this category*	
Clear roles and responsibilities • To what extent have you ensured that your team has the correct skill sets? • To what extent are team members clear about their individual key result areas? • To what extent are team members' workloads accurately reflected in their objectives? *Overall rating in this category*	
Open and honest communication • To what extent do your team members communicate effectively with each other? • To what extent do your team members communicate about feelings? • To what extent do your team members try to adapt their styles when communicating with each other? *Overall rating in this category*	
Rapid response to change • To what extent does your team recognise, define and analyse potential customer problems? • To what extent does your team generate creative problem-solving options? • To what extent does the team adapt to external changes? *Overall rating in this category*	
Effective leadership • How successful are you at 'running interference' so that your team can complete its work and meet customer needs? • To what extent are you providing relevant feedback to team members? • To what extent are you continually motivating team members? *Overall rating in this category*	

Recognising achievements

The manager can help to sustain long-term focus and motivation by instituting and implementing effective reward and recognition systems.

> By providing rewards and recognition to internal service providers, it is possible to raise excitement and commitment to a service culture.

There is a temptation, when the customer service initiative is performing well, to leave well alone. Unfortunately delivering outstanding customer service requires consistent recognition of individual and group accomplishments.

Too often, organisations and individuals view achievements as completion of major milestones. Achievements can also consist of multitudes of moments of truth; small successes that occur every single day. These achievements and moments of truth can occur in both the material (getting the work done) and personal (interacting effectively with the customer) service aspects. Although we experience many of these positive moments of truth per day, instead of recognising them and celebrating them we tend to focus on what has not worked, thereby reducing individual confidence and lowering motivation levels.

As we discussed earlier in this chapter, in our society we receive on average six pieces of negative feedback for every one piece of positive. By recognising and celebrating accomplishments, service organisations not only build cohesiveness, but also positively build trust and morale.

In the future keep your eyes open for those positive moments of truth that you can use to build team spirit and therefore ultimately improve customer service. Awareness of these achievements is the first step in being able to celebrate successes.

Celebrating success

Celebrating achievements provides a sense of well-being and builds morale within the company. Celebrating achievements can be as simple as having a pub meal, or as sophisticated as organising an off-site event for team members at an innovative

location. Ideas for celebrations are listed below. The list is by
no means complete!

◆ team dinner
◆ picnic
◆ barbecue
◆ social events after work
◆ give aways such as sweatshirts, T-shirts, water bottles, etc
◆ awards
◆ certificates
◆ service provider of the month
◆ certificates
◆ complimentary time off
◆ celebrate key milestones with cake, cookies, etc
◆ outdoors experiential event
◆ other team training
◆ off-site events.

Exercise

Celebrating achievements:

Step 1   Identify two achievements in delivering outstanding
customer service. They can be smaller moments of truth
or larger project accomplishments.

Step 2   Decide at least *two innovative ways* you will celebrate *each*
achievement.

Case studies: Cleanworks: turning managers into leaders _____

Was the management team made up of leaders or bosses? Cleanworks had the
opportunity to build its management team from scratch. As part of Cleanworks
University, the managers attended a series of skills-building workshops to build
their team leadership and coaching skills. In addition, they were also responsible
for facilitating key subjects.

The curriculum (Figure 25) therefore involved additional training in facilitation
skills and a train-the-trainer process for specific modules. The company believed
this approach would help ensure that managers really were able to 'walk the talk'
and would become leaders.

Case Study: Kitchen Barn: turning managers into leaders

Was the management team made up of leaders or bosses? The management
team, as we have discussed in Chapter 5, was already acting as leaders in the
customer service initiative by facilitating many of the programmes.

Step in process	Skills and knowledge required	Resources suggested
Introduction to team work	Knowledge ◆ definition of a team ◆ benefits of teams ◆ challenges in teams ◆ stages in team development ◆ characteristics of high-performing teams	Basics of team performance ◆ one day ◆ presented by EM-Power ◆ all management team attends ◆ every participant receives a workbook ◆ session is interactive with exercises and group discussions
Becoming a leader	Knowledge ◆ leader versus manager ◆ team leadership defined ◆ coaching model Skills ◆ feedback skills ◆ giving developmental feedback ◆ motivation techniques ◆ coaching skills ◆ setting team direction ◆ objective setting ◆ performance review	Leadership ◆ two days ◆ presented by EM-Power ◆ all managers attend in one session ◆ every participant receives a workbook ◆ session is interactive with exercises and group discussions ◆ managers define a future action plan
Becoming a facilitator	Knowledge ◆ communication process ◆ facilitation versus teaching Skills ◆ presentation skills ◆ building group interaction techniques ◆ dealing with difficult groups ◆ designing an effective message ◆ using visual aids	Facilitation skills ◆ two days ◆ presented by EM-Power ◆ all managers attend in one session ◆ every participant receives a workbook ◆ every manager makes three videotaped presentations and receives feedback
Train-the-trainer	Knowledge ◆ programme models ◆ learning points ◆ techniques to observe Skills ◆ facilitation skills ◆ building group interaction techniques ◆ presenting the programmes	Train-the-trainer ◆ two days ◆ presented by EM-Power ◆ every participant receives a leader's guide ◆ every manager facilitates part of the programme ◆ group discussion on learning points

Fig. 25. Sample curriculum: turning managers into leaders.

Achieve the objectives: intervening to support customer service

The management team of district managers and regional managers had played an integral role in setting service objectives and standards for their stores, as described in Chapter 7. Their role became pivotal in intervening in the technical data arena so that their teams could provide customer service. The traditional market of kitchen and housewares had a thorough training manual and plenty of written documentation to which sales associates could refer. However, selling furniture required different technical data and more in-depth knowledge of such things as window coverings, wood, beds, etc. None of this information was available in a clear, easily understandable format.

The district managers created a proposal, allotted funds and instituted an in-depth, modular technical training programme that was rolled out to all store personnel over a six-month period. Some of the material was taught in group sessions, often by vendors. Much was in self-teach modules, with tests that the students reviewed with their managers.

The implementation of this programme was an outstanding example of how managers can intervene, from behind the scenes, to help in the external service delivery process.

Develop the individuals: feedback, coaching and motivation

The district managers used the feedback and motivation log for each employee. At weekly conference calls they would discuss one specific success from each district, associated with the one sales associate responsible, as a way of providing unconditional, positive, verbal feedback. The group constantly offered awards for exceptional service, such as free products, single-item focus competitions (SIFs) and, at the annual conference, a sales associate of the year award would be presented.

Gary, as the leader of the entire process, walked the talk and was visible in reinforcing the concepts and providing personalised feedback for exceptional service.

Build the team: the SCORE assessment

Each district team, and then the team within each store, completed the SCORE assessment within a four-week time frame. This assessment was then used in varying ways:

◆ Each district compared the SCORE ratings for each store. Not only did this provide an indication of the teams that were motivated, but there was a strong correlation between the team assessment and the perceived competencies of the store managers by the district manager. Not surprisingly, the store managers who were perceived as strong by the district manager normally had strong teams and vice versa. This tended to validate the district manager's opinion.

◆ Occasionally, the district manager's assessment of the store manager was different from the team's SCORE. For instance, one of the store managers was not well respected, but the team rated itself very highly. This gave the district manager an opportunity to discuss with the team members the reasons for their ratings. In her research she discovered that the store manager was really doing a good job: there had been just one conflict with one of the merchandising managers, which had coloured the store manager's credibility.

◆ Different districts within the same region also compared their results, with the same outcome. It provided the regional manager with an additional source of data about the performance of her regional managers.

◆ As a result, many of the stores initiated a greater focus on strategy, and planned specific store events to build trust and communication within the teams.

Case Study: Internet Express: turning managers into leaders

Was the management team made up of leaders or bosses? Many of the managers in Internet Express were young with no direct management experience. In such software companies, working at the organisation for more than two years normally means promotion to a management role! Such is the dynamic nature of the business.

As a result most of the managers were very technically-oriented, with a limited understanding of the complexity of managing large teams. In addition, because of the relative absence of systems and procedures, many of the managers were spending much of their time fighting fires and reacting, versus focusing on more proactive management responsibilities.

Arthur recognised this challenge and undertook several approaches to help his team become leaders:

◆ He asked the training company that had presented the Managing Customer Perceptions programme to develop and roll out a coaching programme to his managers.

◆ He consciously went outside the company to recruit some individuals from other organisations to add more balance to his management team.

◆ He contracted with a consultant in the short-term, to provide some 'instant-depth' in managing a support function. This consultant was able to work with the existing management team and suggest a range of improvements, resulting in new ideas, as well as the management team learning at the same time.

◆ He made some tough decisions in terms of changing the job roles of two individuals who were struggling with the complexity of managing large teams. One he managed to reassign as a project manager. The other decided to move to another start-up where he could make more of an impact.

Achieve the objectives: intervening to support customer service

One of the biggest barriers to delivering outstanding customer service for the technical support group was the release of products by the engineering group that appeared to be 'riddled with bugs'. The management team realised that the technicians could only do so much on the phone if the quality was seriously lacking.

Each member of the management team picked one of the product areas, and made it their priority to build closer working relationships with the development group responsible for that product, while also formalising service level agreements (as discussed in Chapter 7). In this way, they not only ensured a greater access to development engineers to resolve difficult problems, but they were also able to get a 'heads-up' on future issues. The support team could then institute some sort of proactive fix, such as a patch, a work-around, etc and avoid some of the customer frustrations.

Develop the individuals: feedback, coaching and motivation

The leadership team established a standard call-monitoring worksheet to ensure that the skills taught in the programme were reinforced on a regular basis. The standard was established that all technical support engineers should have one call a month monitored anonymously (the engineer was not aware that the manager was listening in). Although this did not sound like a heavy commitment, managers found that they would have to listen to several calls before they were able to listen to a call when the rep was able to practice the full range of skills on the assessment.

Initially the engineers were resistant to the call monitoring because they believed it implied a criticism of their current performance. When they started to receive positive feedback and rewards (night on the town for the best call in a month), they reduced their negativity and began to compete on who could do best!

In addition, the managers conducted role-plays on a regular basis in staff meetings so that the team as a whole could continue to share experiences and provide each other with feedback.

Build the team: the SCORE assessment

When the team completed the SCORE assessment, they discovered that the customer service strategy was still unclear to many of the team members, despite the efforts that had been made to communicate it. They therefore initiated a new communications campaign that included posters, cards, T-shirts and sweatshirts to spread the word again.

The SCORE assessment also indicated that the leadership team was divided by conflicts between two functional groups and their managers. Arthur invested in taking the team off-site where he combined a strategy session with a team-profiling seminar. The team was profiled using temperament and the Myers Briggs Type Indicator (described in the book *Turning Team Performance Inside Out*). This data provided an objective framework from which to understand the individual differences among team members, and communication and teamwork improved as a result. _____

Discussion points

1. To what extent are your managers acting as leaders in implementing a customer service improvement initiative? How far do they lead rather than direct? How many 'old-school' managers are there who prefer telling rather than influencing?
2. To what extent are the mangers establishing customer service objectives and standards (achieve the objectives)? How regularly are they reviewing these standards and objectives?
3. What else can you do to help the managers develop as customer service coaches (develop the individual)? Do they need specific training in coaching skills? Providing positive feedback? Practising the service delivery skills themselves?
4. To what extent are the teams responsible for delivering service to the internal and external customer performing effectively? Have you conducted the team assessment exercise to evaluate the team SCORE? What could be done to raise team cohesiveness, in order to improve service effectiveness?
5. What else could you do to celebrate successes? What type of reward and recognition systems could you implement to help to sustain the customer service focus?

Summary

In this chapter you have learned about the most important steps to turn your managers into customer service leaders.

- You have reviewed the differences between more traditional managers or bosses and the customer service leader.
- You have seen that being a leader involves being able to lead not just direct, engage the team, have an attitude of 'we' not 'I', but at the same time do real work (serve a customer!), get the team excited and yet still focus on concrete customer service results.
- An effective customer service leader is able to achieve the objectives, develop the individual and build the team.
- Achieving the objectives involves the regular setting and measuring of customer service standards and objectives, together with intervening behind the scenes to help allow the team space to meet customer needs.
- Developing the individual involves providing a balance of positive and developmental feedback, through physical, mental, conditional and unconditional feedback and providing regular coaching.
- Building the team involves assessing the team SCORE and creating strategies to improve team performance. A dysfunctional team is far less likely to exceed customer expectations.
- Managers can help to reinforce the customer service culture by rewarding exemplary performance and celebrating large and small successes.
- The managers are the 'make or break' element in delivering outstanding customer service. All the effort completed in the earlier chapters will be negated if they do not act as role models for the customer service philosophy. Successful companies take active steps to train their managers as customer service leaders and reinforce that positive behaviour.

*Delivering
outstanding
customer
service is
an ongoing
process*

CHAPTER 11

Delighting the Customer

A s we have seen, delivering outstanding customer service requires a clear customer service strategy, effective internal standards and processes, customer-focused people using competent interpersonal skills, continuous improvement and managers who lead the initiative. In this summary we will share some stories of organisations that have implemented these ideas and have delighted their customers. The same message remains, however – delighting the customer is an ongoing process. It never ends.

> Exceeding customer expectations and 'going the extra mile' can leave a memorable impression that the customer talks about time and time again.

It is these types of stories that create a reputation in the marketplace for exceptional service and help to build long-term viability for business. Below are a few examples of companies that have built their success on their reputation for customer service.

- The department store chain in the US, Nordstrom, is a premium priced retailer but has grown enormously on the strength of its customer service stories. Their willingness to refund money when any customer complains could be questioned because technically it 'encourages crooked customers'. In reality, for the one customer who may take advantage there are 99 who will tell everyone they know about the quality of the service they received. One particular story, about refunding a customer for balding tyres (they don't sell tyres) made the front page of the Wall Street Journal: quite a return on investment for the cost of a set of tyres.
- Federal Express gained a reputation for its employees going above and beyond to meet customer needs. Stories of employees pulling victims from aeroplane crashes, spending

off-duty hours tracking down missing addresses, and going above and beyond to deliver packages have helped Federal Express create a market niche for itself, even with tough competition.

◆ The Ritz Carlton hotel chain has created a niche for itself in meeting business travellers' needs, by a concentrated focus on all aspects of service quality.

However, legendary service is not restricted to large chains. Small companies can also delight the customer. Think of those situations such as small restaurants where you eat regularly greet you by name, local copy shops offer advice at no charge to tidy up a newsletter, your coffee shop makes your coffee for you without asking what you want. As a customer, receiving exceptional service is a rewarding experience. Let's finish with my favourite story of being delighted as a customer.

Nick's restaurant in Maui at the Kea Lani Hotel prides itself in delighting its clientele. One of the examples is when it 'spikes its customers'.

Imagine yourself sitting in a restaurant. You are trying to decide what wine would go best with dinner. You are talking to your partner debating the various merits of different bottles. The manager comes to the table to take your order (this alone is unusual on a Saturday evening). You tell your wine selection to him – lo and behold, he brings the bottle of wine that you have selected from behind his back. You have just been spiked!

◆ Such a moment of truth required a series of interconnected actions:
  – A leader committed to exceeding customer requirements.
  – A clear strategy on delivering exceptional service.
  – A process to listen to individual customers as they discussed their wine choice.
  – People who were committed and rewarded by exceeding customer expectations.
  – Constant review of processes to ensure no stone was left unturned in delighting the customer.

We have quoted this story to many people as an example of a small organisation that made a commitment to customer service and delighted the customer. Wouldn't you like your customers to say the same thing about your business?

If your answer is yes – the answer is in your hands. Follow the steps in the book and exceeding your customer expectations will become one of your company's differentiators in the market place. Good luck in this process.

Further Reading

If It Ain't Broke, BREAK IT, Robert J. Kriegel and Louis Patler,
Warner Books, 1999

Direct From Dell. Michael Dell, Harperbusines, 1999

The Brain Book, Peter Russell, Routledge, 1979

Service America: Doing Business In the New Economy, Warner
Books, 1995

Moments of Truth, Jan Carlzon, HarperCollins, 1989

Getting Past No, William Ury, Bantan Doubleday Dell
Publications, 1993

Getting Results! The Secret of Motivating Yourself and Others,
Michael LeBoeuf, Berkeley Publications Group, 1994

Do What You Are, Paul D. Tieger and Barbara Barron-Tieger, Little
Brown & Co, 1995

*What America Does Right: Learning From Companies That Put
People First,* Robert H. Waterman, New York, Norton, 1994

The Age of Unreason, Charles Handy, Harvard Business School
Press, 1991

Getting To Yes: Negotiating Agreement Without Giving In, Roger
Fisher, William Ury, Bruce Patton, Penguin, 1991

The Seven Habits of Highly Effective People, Stephen R Covey,
Simon & Schuster, 1989

The Wisdom of Teams, J. Katzenbach & D. K. Smith, New York,
HarperCollins, 1993

*Language Within Language: Immediacy, a Channel in Verbal
Communication,* Morton Wiener, Albert Mehrabian, Irvington
Publications, 1968

*The 5 Pillars of TQM: How to Make Total Quality Management
Work For You,* Bill Creech, Plume, 1995

Turning Team Performance Inside-Out, Susan Nash, Davis Black
Publishing, 1999

Games Teams Play, L. Berdaly, McGraw Hill, New York, 1996

Index